RACHEL'S RAFT

RACHEL KELLEY

To my loving and ever-so-funny husband, Michael,
to my six beautiful children who have been God's
mouthpiece to me many times, and to the army who has
read, edited, prayed, and most importantly
… believed.

"In the last days, God says, I will pour out my Spirit on all people. Your sons and daughters will prophesy, your young men will see visions, your old men will dream dreams."

Acts 2:17 NIV

Prologue

I have good news, and I have to share it with you.

Good news? No, let me take that back. It's better than that. It's great news. Life-changing news. "Take your shoes off and step back; this is holy ground" kind of-news (Exodus 3:5, paraphrased).

It is truth. A truth I didn't know existed until God awakened it deep down inside me.

The God of Old is the God of Today.

Do you hear what I am saying?

The God of Old is the God of Today.

Yes, He is. That is Him.

The God who parted the Red Sea (Exodus 14:21-22) and annihilated entire troops with songs of praise (2 Chronicles 20) is still moving miraculously today.

Jesus Christ, His son, who came to earth and performed miracles—healing, casting out demons, raising people from the dead (Matthew 8, 9, 10:8)—is alive and well in our time.

The Holy Spirit who releases visions and words of prophecy to men and women (Joel 2:28) is still moving as the Mighty Rushing Wind (Acts 2:2).

Yes, that's the One. The One who is still moving supernaturally, even today.

How do I know this? I have seen it. I have experienced it. I have witnessed it.

Before God began working miracles in my life, He began working on *me*. And, oh my goodness, did it hurt. This process of working on me hurt so bad that sometimes the first thing I would do in the morning was roll out of bed and go directly to the floor on my face in prayer.

But what I didn't understand at the time was God was preparing me to receive His miracles. He had to remove my pride and my self-reliance so that I'd be willing to step out in faith for Him. After I'd been stripped of pride and stripped of myself, I didn't care how crazy His directions were. I didn't care how I looked when I stepped out in faith. My experiences helped me to move forward in faith and gave me strength to say "yes" to His instructions. How I got to a place of receiving His miracles was almost unbearable at times, but His Holy Spirit gave me the strength and power I needed to get through the "stripping process."

So, what does this have to do with a Miraculous God, you ask?

Well, after about ten years of being emptied of myself, I saw God move in ways I'd only read about. I don't know if I'd ever thought about dreams, visions, or prophecy. I was raised in a charismatic church, so I'd observed such things in others' lives but not in my own. But it had been such a long time since I'd seen the miraculous ways of the Holy Spirit, and it had been so long since I'd heard His voice. I didn't even know if I believed that He spoke through dreams, visions, and prophecy anymore. I felt out of touch with Him.

But, that all changed during a very miraculous season of my life.

This is my story...

CHAPTER 1
Summer 2015

It was a sweltering summer day as my husband Michael and I were driving in Mountain View, Arkansas where we had moved a year prior. My birthday was approaching, so I prayed and asked God for a miraculous gift as I had done for several years; each year I witnessed His faithfulness in personal answers, and I anticipated His answer that year, too. His wonders never cease. As we passed a church marquee, I read, "The king's heart is like channels of water in the hand of the Lord; He turns it wherever He wishes. Proverbs 21:1" (NASB).

"Wonder what God has in mind for this weekend?" I thought as we drove past it.

We'd moved to the small tourist town when Michael was offered a job performing at a local theater. He'd spent several years traveling as a vocal impressionist and comedian and was thrilled when the opportunity came to use his gifts and talents in one location. We packed up our home in Tennessee and, with our four children, took on the new adventure. Upon our arrival, the Lord placed on my heart a desire to write a book, a memoir. I'd written several children's books before we moved, but all of a sudden, I had an overwhelming desire to get our trials and struggles and God's faithfulness out in one manuscript. We were pulled to a small Baptist church through a possible job offer where, unbeknownst to us, the author John Grisham's family attended. At one point, I'd gotten to a stopping place in my book, and miracles starting erupting like a fireworks show, many surrounding John Grisham himself. So much so that I knew the story was personal to Grisham and that the Lord wanted me to deliver my manuscript directly *to* him.

The day after my birthday, I cleaned out our homeschool books and supplies and ordered curriculum for our upcoming year. When Saturday arrived, I asked Michael if he wanted me to go down to the town square with him to pass out brochures.

"Yeah, I always like having someone with me."

He left, and after I was dressed, I drove down to meet him. We spent an hour meeting tourists and passing out pamphlets for his show.

"Alright, I think that's good. Let's go home and eat. Then I gotta go to work."

"Wanna ride with me?" I asked.

"Nah, that's okay. I need my car."

"Okay, well, I'll walk you to your car," I said as I stood across the street from my own.

We had walked a few steps when we saw friends from church.

"Well, hey! How are you?"

We exchanged hugs and talked with them for a few minutes. Then one of them said, "I just came from the church. The Grisham family is in town, and they were having a small, private luncheon over there, so I helped get it together."

A pit formed in my stomach. We talked a few more minutes, and when she left I asked Michael, "Okay, so do you think I should try to take my manuscript to him? I mean God has shown me, like He always does. I think if I wait, I'll miss my opportunity."

"Yes, take it now. God will give you the strength."

I called Michelle, one of my closest friends who had read every word of my on-going memoir, on my way home to ask her to pray for me. And she said, "You know what? Last night when I was in the bath, I had this overwhelming feeling of needing to intercede for you. So, I did. I was thinking about how you've been down this road for a while now, and I asked God to complete it. I even prayed, 'Lord, finish this tomorrow. Tomorrow, Lord.' Those were my exact words. So, yes, I think you should take it now."

She prayed for me before we hung up, and I went inside to print off a few minor changes. I put on clean clothes, brushed my hair and my teeth, and while it printed, I turned on the song, "Brave" by Bethel.[1]

As I sang, "For You make me brave. You call me out beyond the shores into the waves. You make me brave. No fear can hinder now the promises You've made," I stood in my bedroom, looking at my words on paper, thanking the Lord for what He'd done in my life.

When I was ready to leave, I asked the Lord for a verse before I walked out the door.

"Lord, give me something..."

"*Psalm 27:3*"

---

[1] Cook, Amanda. "You Make Me Brave." *You Make Me Brave*. Bethel Music, 2014, Track 1.

I grabbed my Bible and turned to the passage which read, "Though a host encamp against me, My heart will not fear; Though war arise against me, In spite of this I shall be confident" (Psalm 27:3, NASB).

"Help me be confident, no matter what," I prayed as I picked up my purse, placed my manuscript inside of it, and walked out the door.

As I drove down the mountain, I reminded myself of my daughter's vision a year prior. "Mom, I just had a vision," she'd said one afternoon. "You were standing in front of the church giving John Grisham your book. But, Mom, you were crying really hard, so don't wear any mascara when you deliver it." I'd never heard her say anything like it before. This word from the Holy Spirit reached the deepest part of my soul, and it stayed with me. I remembered how I was thankful for how God was speaking to me in new ways and giving me clear direction. Remembering this comforted me and helped me move forward with courage, even with nerves ablaze and palms dampened with sweat.

Parking on the side of the street, I prayed again then thought about what I'd say. I walked up slowly, breathing deeply…then pulled on the front door of the building. Walking down the hallway, I noticed a few people sitting at a table, one of those being John Grisham. I'd never met him, but I knew it was him.

Approaching the table, I began to make small talk with the ones I knew when he stood up, "Hello, I'm John Grisham," he said as he reached out his hand.

"Hi, I'm Rachel Kelley," I said as I shook his.

He was warm and friendly—someone I could have sat down with and played a hand of cards or had a cup of coffee.

"It's nice to meet you," he said.

"Nice to meet you, too."

I exchanged greetings with the others realizing I'd arrived at the end of the meal and the guests were gathering their belongings to leave. I felt awkward and rushed as someone I vaguely recognized from church walked towards me, so I took a few steps backwards toward the lobby. We exchanged introductions and a bit of small talk when I realized I had to get out the most pertinent information and quickly!

"Look, I am sure this looks crazy, and you cannot imagine how awkward I feel right now. I have a manuscript I need to give to John Grisham, more like a message really... The miracles in this book, they've surrounded him," I paused nervously, "and I believe I'm supposed to give it to him." I anxiously fumbled with my purse and pulled it out.

The man went on to say it was not a good time and I should take it to someone else if I needed help with publication.

"Please understand this is really uncomfortable for me. I could not feel more awkward than I do in this moment, but I believe this is what the Lord wants me to do."

But his words to me remained the same: take it elsewhere.

By the time he'd finished talking with me, the room had cleared out, and I was left with my book in my hands. In complete deflation, my shoulders sank as did my spirit. "Okay," I paused, "I know this looks crazy. I didn't ask to be here—it's just where God has led me. You have no idea how difficult this journey has been for me. How difficult it has been to place this work in his hands."

"Ma'am, if you are looking for a wall, this is it. Go another direction."

A wall.

In complete surprise, I fidgeted with the papers and tried to act like I was okay. Was I dreaming? Had God really brought me this far only to leave it unfinished once more?

The man went on to thank me for coming by and wished me the best with my work, but by the time I got into my car, the Grisham family was completely gone.

"Whoa, I never saw that coming," I thought as I placed my manuscript in the seat. I was completely shocked. I couldn't imagine how God was going to pull this off when I'd just been standing in the same room with him. How would I ever have that opportunity again? I felt all the breath leave my body.

"Okay, Lord, I obeyed. Give me my next steps."

I turned down Main Street and headed back up Dodd Mountain.

CHAPTER 2
Eight Years Earlier
Pulaski, Tennessee

"Hey babe, I'm going to run to the store and pick up a gift for Mom for Mother's Day real quick. I'll only be gone a few minutes; I can leave the kids, right?"

It was Mother's Day weekend. Michael and I had been married four years, and I had just given birth to our second child, Micah. We were living in Tennessee, and I was planning a trip home to Texas for a wedding.

I needed to get my mom a gift for the upcoming holiday. I asked Michael if I could run to Wal-Mart to get the new Barbara Streisand CD—my mom was a huge fan.

He agreed, so I grabbed my purse and keys and headed to the store. After I picked up the gift and a few groceries, I came home and pulled into our sloped driveway, which was on the side of the house, and parked next to Michael's car. We lived off the highway, and I noticed how the traffic seemed abnormally busy that afternoon. Pulling into my usual spot, I got out of my car, but it continued to roll forward and while aiming downward towards the street. Thinking quickly, I lunged back into the car to try to throw the gear shift into park.

That is when the unthinkable happened.

My car continued to roll until it pinned me up against Michael's car.

"Oh God. Oh God, help."

It was so sudden. I couldn't even comprehend what had happened when I realized half of my body was lying on the driveway and the other half was inside the car. I looked down and saw the floorboard of my car pressing in on me directly below my ribs.

I was no longer able to breathe.

I took a breath, and the car inched in closer. I took another breath and felt the floorboard push further into my chest. There was no hope of exhaling. There was only inhaling. And with each breath in, there were none coming out. Each one I took made me think I was that much closer to my last. Looking down, I saw the car squeezing in.

"Oh God, help me!" I cried out as the pressure began to overtake my body.

The weight of the vehicle was overwhelming. I twisted to one side, and the bottom half of my body did not move. I twisted the other way and pushed with all my might, and the car did not budge. Twisting and turning with everything in me, I still hadn't realized the magnitude of the situation I was now in.

"Help! Help!" I screamed as I looked through the windshield, only able to see the leaves on the trees.

A million thoughts ran through my mind.

"No one is ever going to see me down here on the ground like this; no one can hear me either, not with all this traffic."

I tried to push with all my might.

"I'm going to die right here in my driveway while my family's inside the house."

It was all so abrupt; I didn't even realize what was happening. I went from getting out with groceries to suffocating to death.

I continued to turn and twist in order to free myself from the car, but it was useless. Basically, I was the only thing keeping the cars from colliding, or I was the only thing keeping my car from going on into the street. There was no way I was getting out of this.

"Help!" I yelled. "Oh, God, I'm going to die. God, help me, please. I can't die now."

Then I heard a voice say,

"Lay on the horn..."

I was in the perfect position to lay on the horn—I pressed in on it and did not stop, and that's when I saw the top of the gate swing open and Michael come running toward me.

"Help! Help me! If you don't get this car off of me, I'm going to die! Please," my voice fading, "I'm suffocating; I'm about to die…"

He looked at me through the windshield, clenching his teeth.

"Please, I'm suffocating; get this off me!" I yelled, using what little oxygen I had.

He reached under the car and pulled with all his might, to no avail. Pulling and pulling, he used all his strength but was still not able to lift the car.

"Help! Help! Someone, please help me!" He screamed at the top of his lungs—trying to overcome the noise of the road.

Panicked, I saw that the only one I thought could help was not strong enough to do it on his own.

"He can't do it; he can't help me," I thought as my frame weakened, my hope diminished. "I'm still going to die."

I looked in my rearview mirror to see a young man suddenly standing behind my car, talking on the phone.

"Get him! Get him!" I screamed, my voice fading.

Michael yelled and motioned for the young man to come around to the front of the car. He put down his phone and ran around to the front of the car, both lifting with all their might, but they still couldn't do it.

In that moment, all I could think about was how Michael was ever going to able to raise our two babies by himself. Micah was breastfeeding. How would he eat? Caroline was not even two yet. Thoughts of my babies played through my mind as if they would be my last earthly memories. My thoughts turned to Michael. How would he cope? Could he take care of them as a single dad? The thoughts went around and around in my head as if they were spinning, or I was; I didn't know which one.

"What if I died in my driveway? My husband and my kids would see me die this way... *how gruesome.*"

My thoughts were back on the two men who were now both screaming for someone to stop, back on what was happening in real time, when a truck pulled up. A man and a woman jumped out and ran over to the car. I could barely see them now, as I was drifting back and forth from looking at the car crushing my abdomen, thinking of death, and praying for God to rescue me. I seemed to be living in slow motion.

"I don't know how much longer I'll last." My body was weary, aching in agony to get one…more…breath…

Suddenly, something changed—a release.

I felt my body slam against the pebble stones on the driveway, my arms crash down to my side, my lungs release to find the oxygen they desperately needed. I looked up at the people standing around, the ones looking down on me with fear and relief all wrapped up in one expression. When I glanced up again, I saw my dentist, whose office was across the street from our house, standing in our driveway.

"Rachel, are you okay?"

I stared at him.

"Rachel, what year is it?"

"Two thousand and seven."

"Rachel, who's the President?"

"Bush," I replied.

I heard the sirens, and I knew they were coming for me. By this time, several people had gathered around. The ambulance pulled up as I noticed my neighbor coming out of my house, holding Micah on her hip and holding Caroline's hand. The paramedics wheeled the stretcher up to the driveway.

"Take them inside!" I yelled. "I don't want them to see me like this," I exclaimed as I saw the confusion in Caroline's expression and her hands stretched out towards me.

The EMT worker approached with a clipboard and started asking me questions.

"I was sandwiched between the cars. I wasn't breathing," I explained as I used my sleeve to wipe the tears from my face. He came over to me and started wrapping things around my wrist and arms while listening to my heart. Loading me onto the stretcher, I looked at the crowd that had now gathered in our yard. He turned to Michael, "Sir, you can come with us."

The scene of the accident where I was sandwiched between two cars.

"Can you tell me what happened?" the EMT asked as he continued to hook me up to machines.

"I don't know. I got out of the car, and I don't know if I didn't put it in park or what, but it kept rolling. I dove back in to put it into park, and it pushed me up against the other car," I cried.

The hospital was only a mile from our house, so we were there by the time I finished explaining what I remembered. After they wheeled me into a room, the doctor walked in. "First, we are going to do an MRI to see if you have any internal bleeding."

The news startled and disturbed me.

"Internal bleeding? That doesn't sound good," I whispered to Michael, who stood by my side holding my hand.

After the MRI, I waited in the hospital room when the door cracked open and in walked a solemn Dr. Gahn.

"Mrs. Kelley," he said, "Your MRI shows internal damage and bleeding. A normal enzyme level is about 30; yours is over 3,000."

I had no idea what that meant, but I knew it wasn't good news. My heart raced.

"What is he saying?" I thought. "I'm here. I didn't die in the driveway. I should be fine."

"There's a helicopter coming from Vanderbilt to get you."

"What?" I asked.

"If you need surgery or transfusions, you'll need to be at Vanderbilt."

"Surgery or blood transfusions? Why?"

He went on to explain when I felt my mind totally tune out. I was seeing his mouth move, watching words come out, but I was not comprehending anything.

"I should be okay, right?" I asked. "Tell me that I'm going to be okay."

"That is our goal," he replied.

"That's your goal? So, I might not make it?"

"There's a helicopter on its way; it'll be here in twenty minutes."

I started to cry. I wanted to go home. Wanted to see my babies. Wanted to kiss and hold them and love on them. How did it come to this? I heard a knock on the door. A few of our friends had come to pray, and as they circled around me, I laid on the stretcher trying to wrap my mind around all that had happened in the last few hours. Taking Michael's hand, I looked at him and saw the intensity of his eyes and felt the desperation in his requests. They had just finished when two men dressed in uniforms walked in. The blue jumpsuits with bold, intricate patches on their shoulders were evidence of their life or death mission.

"Rachel, we're here to take you to Vanderbilt," one of the men said while smiling warmly.

After Michael and I signed the papers and filled in the necessary information, my friend took my hand, looked me straight in the eye, and whispered, "Remember, the Lord is with you."

And with that thought in my mind, I saw the ceiling tiles above me, my husband and friends behind me, and the door open in front of me. I saw the night sky above me, the stars all in array, and then I heard the whizzing of the propellers.

"One, two, three. Up."

My stretcher settled in the helicopter that would take me to Nashville. Doubts of my future filled my mind, so I decided to start making deals with God.

I thought about laying down the size of my family and the content of my days. All I wanted was to live; God could have the rest of my life if only I could live to see it. "Ok, God. Want me to surrender? I will. I'll have however many kids You want me to." I also thought about forgiveness. I needed to be forgiven for complaining. "I've griped about being a stay at home mom. Oh God, I'm sorry; You've given me a beautiful life. Please don't take it from me now."

I spent the night in the trauma intensive care unit separated by curtains from the other five patients in the room, and the next morning I talked to a psychiatrist who came to counsel each one of us.

"How long will it haunt my thoughts?" I asked, panicking as I thought about dying.

"You know, I've been here for nine years, and you're only the second person I've seen who's been pinned between two cars. The other case was a lady who was pinned in at the knees in a parking lot—so I've not seen a situation like yours; it's rare. However, it's normal for your mind to play it over and over," he said kindly, "But as time passes, it will become an easier memory to live with."

They continued to observe me and watch my vitals, but it became more apparent that my health was good and my condition was stable. So, before noon that day, my doctor signed the orders for me to be released—to say I was overcome with gratefulness would be an understatement. My cousin called while I was being released, and she told me while she'd been putting on her make-up that morning, the Lord spoke to her, "I have great plans for Rachel."

And after my near-death miracle, I believed it to be true.

CHAPTER 3

The years following the accident were tumultuous to say the least. Early in our marriage, I worked for Dominican Sisters, or Catholic nuns, and it was during that time I felt convicted about our family planning. The Sisters taught against birth control and advocated natural family planning, but ultimately, they believed the decision about the number of children a couple has should be up to the Lord. God wanted me to surrender that area to Him, which led to the birth of our third child, Camille. I kinda-sorta obeyed, but I wasn't ready to give God complete control of our family planning. Not yet.

Michael was working for a school in Nashville, and they were experiencing financial difficulty. So, while I felt God wanted to bless our family with children, it didn't seem like He was providing for us the way I wanted Him to—financially. Looking back now, He was providing other things—humility, reliance on Him, growth of prayer life— but I could not see that then.

Sister Teresa Benedicta, Caroline, our first daughter, and me

One morning, I woke up early feeling insecure—like I couldn't trust if the school was going to pay us or not. We'd always had a sure foundation of at least a paycheck, but this was weird. We had talked about Michael applying elsewhere, so we started sending out resumes. I checked my e-mail account as well as Michael's.

No new e-mail.

I was hoping one of the resumes would open a door to financial freedom, but nothing. Just silence. And junk mail. I noticed his calendar that was sitting on the floor next to his laptop. I opened it to January—no vocal impersonation comedy gigs, which he was doing as a side job. None for February yet, either.

It was so cold outside. The wind was blowing the single, yellow light that hung at the intersection of Sam Davis and College Streets. Back and forth it blew in the wind. I turned to look out the window by the couch where I was sitting. Placing my Bible in my lap, I sat in silence.

Doubt loomed in my mind. What was going on?

"God, I feel like I'm at the bottom here."

I closed my eyes. I expected to hear something new and freeing. Something that would send my worries out the door and into the chill where they belonged. I sat. I expected God to answer me in a way I could touch and feel—preferably with cold, hard cash in the equation. An e-mail. An interview. I believed we would wake up and have all the answers regarding our income flow. And as I sat, I heard something I never expected. Something that jarred my soul.

"I'm at the bottom. And if you want to be with Me, this is where we are going to hang out."

It was as clear as the mist that had collected on the window screen.

An answer I never anticipated.

It was not what I was looking for. Not what I wanted to hear. I wanted to be rescued that day. I didn't know what He meant—going to the bottom. I didn't know I would claw and scrape the muddy walls all the way down, not free fall. But I knew my answer, in the terms I was anticipating, was not coming anytime soon.

And with that thought in mind, I braced for the descent.

CHAPTER 4

"Mom, there's something on the porch!" my daughter Caroline exclaimed, "Hurry; come get it."

I set the plate back on the table, wiped my hands on the towel, and walked to the front door. Opening the screen door, I saw several bags sitting on the porch, right under the mailbox.

"What in the world? What's all of this?"

My other two kids came rushing to see the surprise.

"Wow, Mommy, look at all this food!" Camille shrieked with excitement.

"Yes, sweetheart, look at all of this." I picked up two bags in each hand. "Come back inside with Mommy, and we can see what all is in here!"

As we unloaded seven bags of groceries, my mind wandered back to a time when I was younger, to a time when my family had struggled, but I remembered nothing like this. I'd never seen anyone leave food on our doorstep.

"Probably because they never did," I thought as I set the last bag on the countertop.

"God, you know I'm grateful. I am," I prayed as I started taking out the groceries and putting them in the cabinet, "but with all that is in me, I can't understand why You're doing this. Why?

I want to say I'm excited and thankful, I do. I am thankful, but Lord, I'm also embarrassed. How come this is what it looks like to follow You? How come You've brought me to a place where people are leaving groceries on my doorstep?"

The financial tension continued to bring Michael and me to our knees over and over. The college had paid him once in February, but they were still behind on the total amount they owed him. Michael knew he could leave the school, but he had nowhere else to go for work. I was filling out resumes online for him with every spare minute I had, and Michael was calling to book his vocal impression shows on his days off and even on his lunch breaks. He booked a few, but he was still receiving some of the same reasons for lack of interest: no funding, in-house artists, budget cuts, and on the list went.

We began to fast, too. God was speaking to us but not in terms of what job to take or when He would give Michael work that would pay. We were hearing:

"Keep going."

"I am with you."

"You've been faithful in the small things; I will put you in charge of many things" (Luke 16:10, paraphrased).

We were asking for material answers and were being given big Spiritual truths. I wanted something more concrete, something more tangible. We questioned me staying at home and Michael performing shows, but we continually felt that the Lord was not releasing us from our positions.

The next day was Bible study, and I was in desperate need of it. I got the kids dressed and drove to our church. My eyes a little puffy from the previous night, I walked in late and sank down in the seat next to a friend.

"You okay?" she asked.

"Not really. Michael isn't getting paid, once again."

A few eyes turned to look at me.

I looked at her prayer request list and saw "The Kelleys" already on it. One lady sitting behind me reached up to give me a hug. Our "adopted grandmother" was already in the room, so I figured she had already told them about our continuing ordeal.

"Oh well, at least they already know."

Then my teacher, Ally, asked, "Rachel, how're ya doing this morning?"

"Not that great. Michael isn't getting paid again."

I could not stop the tears that were already coming. It was all I could say. I couldn't get one more word out.

"We're gonna pray for you guys this morning," she said.

They did, and she continued on with the lesson while I continued to fight the tears. I couldn't concentrate; my mind went from wondering what we were going to do, to what other jobs Michael could apply for, and on to the balance in our account and our growing debt. I couldn't help but question God; why wouldn't He fix it?

When the class was over, I reached for my purse, put my Bible inside of it, and walked toward the door. As I did, two ladies, Sylvia and Jeanette, stopped me.

"Rachel, do you think it'd be okay if we stopped by for a little while?"

My gut dropped.

Sometimes, I didn't know if people were going to help or if they were going to give advice. Beforehand, I thought financial issues could be solved simply by getting another job or asking for a raise. But I was discovering was that it was not that simple. If God was not moving a certain direction, there was no changing Him.

"Uh, sure, that's fine."

"Okay, we'll be by in a few minutes."

I picked the kids up from the nursery and drove home. When they arrived, I invited them in, and we sat down in the living room.

"Kids, go play outside for a few minutes," I said.

"So, tell us how you are doing."

"Well, not that great. I feel like we stepped out years ago in faith and have gone from one crisis to the next. I don't understand what God is doing. Or why He won't help Michael provide for his family."

"What's going on with his paychecks?" they asked.

"The school's funding is in some sort of trouble. No one's getting paid regularly, not even the President. And Michael's side gigs have almost dried up altogether. I feel like we are failing."

Then, ever so sweetly and gently, Sylvia said, "Try not to think of this as a trial, Rachel, think of this as a test. You are not on trial in front of God; He's giving you a test."

Contrary to what I was starting to believe, I was not sitting in the courtroom with an angry judge wondering what crime I had committed and if I would be forgiven. I was sitting in a classroom with a loving teacher being asked to take a test to show a faithful Instructor what I was learning. At times, I felt I was failing miserably. Other times, I felt closer to God than I had in years. He was bringing me to my knees, sometimes even my face, in desperation.

Jeanette, who was sitting on my right, pulled out a piece of paper. "Okay. Tell us everything you need at the grocery store."

And she meant everything—even down to the spices in the cupboard. She made a long list of food and toiletries. "Alright, well, we're gonna go to Wal-Mart; why don't you all come with us?"

"Okay, sure."

"Good, also... there's a consignment sale goin' on right now. We're gonna go over there and get whatever y'all need. Shoes, pants, dresses, even if Michael needs things, we will get 'em. Why don't we go there first; then we'll go to the grocery store?"

"You don't even know how much this means to me." My voice cracked. "Thank you…words can't even describe."

I gathered up the kids and grabbed their coats.

"Why don't you drive us to the consignment sale, and then you can bring us all back to your house for us to get our car?" Jeanette suggested.

That should have clued me in on their next move. Before we turned into the church where the consignment sale was being held, Sylvia said, "Turn in here," and pointed to the gas station. "We're gonna fill up your car."

If Christ appeared to me that day, it was in the form of two sisters from my Bible study. When they bought our family of five clothes, food, and gasoline, they became a tangible force of grace and provision in my life. For with these actions, my two sisters followed this verse perfectly:

> What good is it, my brothers and sisters, if someone claims to have faith but has no deeds? Can such faith save them? Suppose a brother or a sister is without clothes and daily food. If one of you says to them, "Go in peace; keep warm and well fed," but does nothing about their physical needs, what good is it? In the same way, faith by itself, if it is not accompanied by action, is dead (James 2:14-17, NIV).

One thing I was learning was how to tell people how we *really* were. I didn't want to tell people about our problems. I wanted to put on the face, the smile, and a new dress— 'cause as long as we looked okay, people would assume we were okay. But we weren't okay.

God was taking me to an unfamiliar place—a place of seeing His body, His church for what they were: a body. A single organism working for its own good to the glory of God.

I wanted Michael to get a better job, for the vocal impersonation gigs to provide income, or for the school to pay him on time for his work. I wanted God to answer my prayers in a way that would give us safety. But I couldn't make anything happen myself.

I was expecting our fourth child, and one morning while I was getting ready to go to my doctor's appointment, I cried out to God.

"Caroline, go upstairs and get out of your pajamas. And would you mind helping Camille, too?"

I went back into my bedroom to get ready and shut the door.

"God, why are you doing this to me? Why?"

I sat in silence.

"God, please help me. Help me."

I'd been reading Isaiah 54 for a year. It spoke to me over and over, and so I opened my Bible to it once more.

"Do not be afraid; you will not be put to shame.
Do not fear disgrace; you will not be humiliated.
You will forget the shame of your youth
and remember no more the reproach of your
widowhood.
For your Maker is your husband—
the LORD Almighty is his name—
the Holy One of Israel is your Redeemer;
he is called the God of all the earth.
The LORD will call you back
as if you were a wife deserted and distressed in spirit—
a wife who married young,

only to be rejected," says your God.
"For a brief moment I abandoned you,
but with deep compassion I will bring you back.
In a surge of anger I hid my face from you for a moment,
but with everlasting kindness I will have compassion on
you,"
says the LORD your Redeemer (Isaiah 54:4-8, NIV).

Tears filled my eyes.

Then I prayed, "God, in spite of how I feel today, I know
that I'm fearfully and wonderfully made (Psalm 139:14). I know
with all that's in me. I know, God, that You've said children are
a great blessing (Psalm 127:3). I know the shape I'm in right
now, although tired, is the shape you have designed for me at
this time in my life. I'm going to praise You for it. God, I am
obeying You. You've told us to have children, and I'm walking
in that. This daughter, she's Yours, Lord. You're loaning her to
me, but she belongs to You. God, I'm also your daughter (1
John 3:1). You love us both, I know, but please show me. Lord,
I am looking ridiculous to the world right now. And I am about
to look even stupider. Having all these kids. It looks stupid. But
I know, Father, that You did not place me with the Catholic nuns
for nothing. You had a plan for that. And You were
passionately pursuing me then as You still are now. You desire
truth in my inmost parts (Psalm 51:6). Your Word says so. Lord,
this is how I'm expressing truth. Truth that children are a
blessing. Truth that obedience to You comes at a cost (Matthew
6:24) and to the world may seem stupid (1 Corinthians 4:10).
But, that's no reason to lay down my cross. No, never. That
because of You, I will take this cross up and continue to follow
You (Matthew 16:24), no matter what the world thinks or says.
If they hated You, they will hate me (John 15:18-19). If they
made fun of You, they will make fun of me. I'm going on, Lord.

I am continuing on this path. For You've ordained it. It's You and me today, Lord. You and me."

I opened the door and called for the kids to come down the stairs.

"All right everyone, go jump in the car," I said as I picked up my keys and my purse.

When we arrived at the doctor's office, I sat the kids down in the chairs next to the counter where I checked in.

"Good morning, Rachel. How are you?" the receptionist asked.

"Fine, thanks."

"Do you have a new insurance card?"

"Um," I fumbled through my purse, "Yes."

I reached into my wallet and took it from the card pouch.

"Here." I slid it under the glass window.

And in that moment, I was her.

I became her.

The woman that I'd looked down on. The one with all those kids who was having more and couldn't even afford the ones she had. The one who had to rely on other people for help. I was her. And though I had tried to avoid it with everything in me, there was no getting around it. My identity as I once knew it was gone, and a new Rachel was coming forth. A broken Rachel. A Rachel who was learning to follow God, even when it didn't feel good or make sense. Not the way I had thought. Or expected. But the way God had planned all along.

CHAPTER 5

Michael got laid off from his job and began pursuing vocal impressionist shows as a full-time ministry. It was where God led us.

At one of Michael's shows, a businesswoman we admired said I should offer something to sell at his shows. "What

about writing a children's book?" she asked me. I always enjoyed writing, and because I had kids, I thought I could write something children liked. My mom, an artist, was my illustrator, and within a few months, our first book was born. Then our second, a children's devotional. By the time

Michael impersonating Tom Jones
at a ministry fundraiser

we produced our third book, I decided to send letters to agents and call area schools about author visits. It was minimally successful, and the whole process eventually became quite frustrating.

That summer, we drove to Louisiana for one of Michael's shows pulling a trailer loaded down with props, sound equipment, and my children's products. We turned onto a street to find the home that was hosting us, and when we did, the trailer started to slip and got stuck in the mud. Michael alternated between forward and reverse several times—the trailer didn't budge. We all got out of the car, and Michael tried to push it—to no avail. A neighbor came out to help, and when they finally released it from the mud, everyone was dirty and tired. Michael was running late to the show and was stressed when he arrived. Feeling frazzled afterwards, he forgot his computer and had to drive thirty minutes back to the church to get it. After he got the computer, he had to make calls to book more shows.

I was worried about him. It wasn't just this episode; this was the norm for us. He seemed tired and worn out. I called a friend the next morning.

"I'm worried about him. This is a lot on his shoulders."

"You know, I've been thinking about and praying for you guys, too," she paused, "Rachel, I have no idea how y'all are going to keep up at this rate."

"Yeah," I paused, "that's what I'm worried about."

After we hung up, I sat down at their barstool, opened my Bible, and skimmed a few pages. Then, I bowed my head.

"God," I whispered, "You know I'm worried about Michael. He has so much on him, and I don't know how he'll ever keep up."

Then I sat there in silence.

With my eyes still closed, I saw a vision of Michael treading water.

32

"Yes, God, that's Michael. He's treading water."

I saw him, in my mind, treading.

Then, a raft came in.

A raft came in and scooped him up. He was at ease, and he was happy. He had his feet lying on the raft, relaxing; he even had an umbrella drink in his hand.

That was the vision in my mind—a raft that made the treading cease.

"Lord," I prayed, "Send the raft. You know what it is. I ask You to send it, whatever that may be."

It was such a clear picture to me. A raft. Something that would bring us relief from the storm. I asked my mom and my friend, Abigail, to also pray. I told them I didn't know what the raft was; I just knew God needed to send it.

I would continue to pray this prayer myself for sixteen months, never having a clue what it was or how it would arrive but trusting it would.

The shows started slowing down, so Michael applied for several jobs. He found one in Nashville working at a factory. When they cut back hours, I asked if I should book author visits for elementary schools. Our options were slim, so he agreed I should make calls, even though we had whole-heartedly given up on the idea.

Again, and hopefully for the last time, I got in my car to go to the church. Our church was gracious to let us use a Sunday school room when either of us needed to make calls, so I glumly walked down the all too familiar hall to the classroom. The teacher's vinyl seat and the small wooden table looked the same as it did last time—cold. It was a wearisome routine activity for me, and I had no heart left in the effort. But I desperately wanted to help out, so I plugged my laptop into the wall, and I pulled out a sheet of paper for notes.

"Okay. Let's see. What schools have I not yet tried," I thought to myself. "Hendersonville area. I'll call them."

"Good morning. Pleasant Heights Elementary."

"Hi. My name is Rachel Kelley, and I am a children's book author. I was wondering if I might speak with your librarian about a possible school visit."

"Yes ma'am. I'll put you through."

"This is Mrs. Davis. Please leave a message."

"Ah, voicemail," I thought as I left a message.

"Next school," I said as I scrolled through the online lists from the Nashville area.

On and on I went for two hours—leaving messages and speaking with people who didn't seem interested in what I was offering.

And as I was writing down the schools I had called, I heard,

"I want you to share your story."

It was so clear I actually wrote the words on the list of schools that I had tried to reach.

"This is going nowhere. I'm done. And empty."

34

I picked up my laptop, curled up the cord and shoved it into the case. Digging into my purse, I found the keys to the car that would take me back to the same situation, the same house, the same place of weariness.

My case swung over my shoulder, my purse in my hand, I walked down the unlit hallway. And from the depth of me, I asked God, "God, if You still love me, if You still care about me, if You are still in this, I need to know. I need to know today."

Pulling into my driveway, I knew that I was at an all-time low. I walked in through the back door where I found Michael dressed with his hair wet from showering. The kids were running from the living room through the kitchen and the baby was in her highchair, crying.

"Hey! The factory called and said I could come in this afternoon. How were your calls?"

"Not good. No one was interested."

A pit grew in my stomach.

"Well, I've gotta go. Andy, a guy who works on houses, is coming by in a minute to take a look at the wood. Let me know what he says," Michael said.

And with that, I kissed him, told him I loved him, and watched him close the back door.

We'd put our house on the market because we could no longer afford it. The last couple that had looked at it was concerned about termite damage. We'd had two termite inspectors come to look for termites within that time who said we had no sign of termites, so I wasn't worried. But Michael went ahead and hired a repairman to come fix the small section of rotten wood.

I was cutting up food for lunch when I saw Andy walk to the side of the house.

"Good, he's here. He'll fix that small patch, and we'll tell that couple it was nothing," I thought.

Hungrily, the kids came in to grab plates and apple slices as I heard the tearing of the wood.

"He's probably already done."

Then, I heard a knock on the back door.

I opened it.

"Hey, Andy. How are you?"

"Not too good."

Then he held up a piece of wood about a foot long.

"Rachel, I know you've had two termite inspectors come, but if these aren't termites, I'd like to know what they are."

My eyes glazed over. I looked down at the piece of wood. Then, I saw them—short, white-looking ants all over the wood.

"Oh no, Andy. Please tell me you are kidding me. There's no way we have termites."

"I'm going to call an inspector one more time. I know they've told you twice you don't have termites, so I'll get them over here again to see if we can find out what is goin' on."

I stood in disbelief.

"Maybe it's not termites, right, Andy? Maybe it's some bugs or ants. We've had ants before. Surely two different inspectors would have caught it."

"Well, I would've thought so, too, but these sure look like termites," his words only added weight to my already heavy heart.

"I'll call Murray at the pest company and have him come and take a look."

He walked back outside and pulled out his cell phone.

"No way would God do this to me, not today." I thought to myself.

I walked into the dining room and sat down with the kids who were eating happily.

"What did he say, mama?" my son asked.

"Well, we have some bugs living in our wood, and I'm hoping it's nothing serious."

Outside, I could hear Andy pounding and scraping, still removing the damage from the house. A little while later, a white truck pulled up outside. Then, there was a knock on the back door.

"Hey, I'm Murray. I've been looking at your house, and I'm not sure how I missed it before, but you definitely have termites."

My mind reeled.

"You've got to be kidding me...let me see."

I pushed through the inspector and turned the corner, my olive green skirt twirling around my knees.

"Oh God, Oh God. . ."

And as I stared at the remnants of what used to be the side of my house, I got it. I finally got it.

"That's me. It's a picture of me. God, I see it; it's me. This is all that is left of me—studs. You have completely torn me down to the studs. You've stripped me down to this. I see it," I prayed.

At that moment, I knew God was giving me a physical picture of what was happening to me spiritually. Andy had pulled off layer after layer of rotten wood, leaving the interior of our home exposed, the insulation hanging out, and a pile of rotten, termite-ridden wood in a pile.

"You've taken me down to nothing. I have nothing left."

Murray turned to me as the sun started heating my bare shoulders.

"Well, let's talk about different treatment options, ma'am, if that's okay with you. Do you want to stand under that tree?" He pointed to the dogwood tree that was no longer in bloom.

"I think I need to sit down. Can we go inside?" I asked.

We turned toward the house, toward the damage, and walked inside. I took him into the living room and offered him a seat on the couch opposite of mine. It was hard to listen to what he was saying. In my mind I was wondering how I would tell Michael about the termites. How would we pay for it? How extensive was it? A million things were running through my mind.

"Okay, well, we have two different options," Murray begins. "We can treat the entire house assuming you have the holes dug in the concrete already, which I think you might. Or, we can do a section of the house."

"Um, ok," I said still not comprehending it all.

Then, he looked at me intently and asked me this:

"Ma'am, can I change the subject?"

"Yes, please."

He paused then asked, "Do you feel that you are sticking your finger in one hole to find water coming out from another hole? Then you stick your finger there, and the water comes out somewhere else?"

Tears welled up in my eyes as I lifted my heavy head at his words.

"Yes, I feel like that."

"Well, this is what I believe the Lord wants to say to you today. He works all things together for good to those who love the Him and are called according to His purposes (Romans 8:28). I know you might not to be able to see it now, but He will work this out for your good. It's a promise to you today."

And with that, he went back in to the treatment option plans.

I was stunned.

I was trying so hard to hold back the flood of tears that was coming.

It was as if Jesus Christ himself had appeared to me in the form of a termite man and had spoken to me in terms outside earthly reasoning.

When he was done speaking, he got up to inspect the house further and to get the chemicals needed to kill what was left of the destructive insects.

I sat down, my face to the ground, watching as the tears spilled onto the floor.

CHAPTER 6

The birth of our fourth child, Mary Manor, was like a bandage on my aching spirit. We were excited by her birth; she was delightful and brought us a lot of joy—happiness filled my heart. But, at the same time, I noticed something shifting in Michael and me, our talks started changing, they were different. A new level of brokenness. And it concerned me.

My Thursday morning Bible study started a new class— a grief share class. At first I thought I might not relate to the other members in the class, but as our teacher assured us we can grieve all sorts of different things in life, I knew she was talking to me. Any kind of loss—the loss of a spouse, the loss of a child, the loss of a job, the loss of a dream.

"Yes, that's it, the loss of a dream."

I'd lost the passion and zeal that came from knowing God had a plan for me. I'd replaced it with loss of vision and with doubt.

One morning, we gathered in small groups and were encouraged to share what it was we were grieving. One girl was grieving her miscarriage, the other was grieving the loss of her health, and we sat listening, not offering advice, but validating feelings. When the circle turned toward me I admitted, with tears in my eyes, "I'm grieving the loss of a dream, the loss of thinking God called me to something only to feel that He's forgotten about me."

I continued on with my story but felt there was not finality—only uncertainty and confusion. In my mind, I knew He told me He'd never leave me or forsake me (Hebrews 13:5), but when I looked at how I'd followed Him and felt I was left in the cold, I was overcome with sadness.

"What advice bothers you the most, Rachel?" my teacher asked.

"When I tell people my situation, how we've struggled, and they smile and say, 'Yes, but God is good.'"

"You'd like to say, 'If God is so good, then where is the money for groceries this week,'" right?"

"That's it exactly."

One night Michael came home from work, and the kids were in bed. After he ate, we had our usual talk about what we were going to do, as always.

He sat down on the couch and was silent, and I was in the rocking chair, steadily rocking back and forth.

"I don't know what to do anymore," he said. "Maybe it's hopeless."

Silence.

"No. It's not hopeless," I explained as I turned my head to look at him in his eyes.

"I don't know anymore," he paused, "maybe it is."

His shirt hung out. His pants were worn. His hands and fingernails were black from the assembly line work at the factory.

"I think it might be," he added.

Silence.

"I don't know why God gave me a family when He knows I can't take care of them."

"That's not true. You're doing a great job. We have food. We have our house. The kids are happy. We're fine," I said trying to encourage him.

"No, I mean that I can't support you and the kids like you need me to," his voice faded. He lifted his eyes to look at mine, "I think y'all would be better off without me."

"No," I pleaded as I stood up, "you don't mean that."

"I don't know, maybe I do," he said. "Rachel, you're beautiful. If something happened to me, you'd have someone else to take care of you and our kids right away. Someone that could take care of you. Not someone like me."

I ran over and knelt by the couch where he was sitting, took his hands, and looked in his eyes.

"No. You don't mean that. I love you. You only. God has a plan. He does. You can't say that. The kids and I…we don't want someone else. We want you. I don't want you to talk like that. God put you and me together for a purpose. He did."

"I know. I used to believe that," He continued, "But He doesn't open any doors for me. I've tried everything. I've asked everyone I know. You've sent tons of resumes; I've called for shows, the only job I have is not cutting it, and the ones that interview me don't want me. I can't take care of you and the kids."

He paused, "If God doesn't want me doing the things He's put in my heart, then I wish He'd take away the desire. Why would He give me talents and not want me to use them? But it's more than that. I can't take care of my family like I want to."

"Yes, you can. We can do whatever, whatever you want to do."

"No, we can't. We can't sell this house, I can't get a job that supports us—we are stuck," he continued, "Y'all would be better off with my insurance policy than with me."

"No!" I yelled. "No, that's not true! Please don't say that Michael. We love you. I love you. I want you. I don't care if I'm living on the street in a cardboard box. You're my husband; they are my kids. This is our family. Don't talk like that, please!"

"I want to be with you and the kids, just not like this," he said.

"Don't even think about taking your life. It's not the answer, and you know it. Wait. Help is coming. It is. God will rescue us. He will. Don't lose hope. He'll do it."

"No, I know. I'm not going to take my own life. But sometimes it crosses my mind," he cried as he looked at me with watery eyes.

"Yes, I know. It crosses mine, too. But we know that it's never God's answer. Never. There's always hope. There is."

We sat in silence for a moment.

"Keep reminding me of that."

"Let's shake on it. Let's promise each other we'll never take our own lives, no matter how bad it gets," I said with all seriousness.

He reached out his hand and took mine.

"Promise me, we'll never take our own lives, no matter what," I whispered.

"Okay, I won't take my own life."

"No matter what?"

"No matter what."

Our emotions were all over the place. I was dealing with the life of a newborn along with taking care of the other three. I knew I was emotional anyway, but I also knew it was more than hormonal—it was spiritual. Michael gave me a sermon that we listened to over and over. About storms. And what they produce—fruit. And that no matter how violent those storms seem, suicide was never the answer. We listened to it. Then listened to it again.

Michael had interviewed with a college in Missouri, but several days later, he received a letter confirming what we feared—he was not the candidate chosen for the position. With the hopes of a new job gone and with more debt adding up, I was weary.

I had to know. I had to know why I tried to do everything right in my life. Why would I follow all those things I knew God had led me to? Why even try?

"God, You told me to have kids, and I'm having them. You told me to stay at home with them, and I'm doing that, too. And homeschooling. I've supported Michael in what You've called him to do. Why can't You do this? Why won't You do this? Is it too hard to give him a job? Is it too hard for You to let him be successful? I don't believe You're that weak. Are You?" I vented.

Michael was worried. It was becoming unbearable. Sometimes I wanted to walk away from my life. Start over. Another life. At first I thought it was Satan. That Satan was attacking us and we needed to do more spiritual warfare.

"Yes, that's it," I'd think to myself. "We need to bind Satan more, get rid of any idols in the house, fast and pray and march around the house."

But then I'd change my mind.

"No. No way is Satan this strong. This isn't Satan we're fighting. It's God. And when you fight God, there's only one winner, and it's not me," I would think to myself.

The power was too great. The power was too strong. It was like God Himself was blocking every door. With no way around.

"God, what kind of example are we to the lost?" I asked. "Who would follow You when they look at our life?"

I knew there were people who were worse off than us, though. I knew that. People who were facing dreadful diseases and sleeping on the streets. I'd met many of them in our travels. People who were homeless and people who had lost children and spouses—lost loved ones in their lives. I knew that. And while it made me feel thankful momentarily to know I was not in their

46

shoes, the feeling faded when I was, once again, overcome with our situation. And what united all of us who were suffering was the sinking feeling of hopelessness. Wondering if there was an answer. Was there anyone who cared? Would it ever turn a corner? Or was this how it all played out? I'd go to sleep thinking about my situation and wonder if tomorrow it would be different. Then, I'd wake up, realize I'd had a temporary escape in the night but was faced with it again. Sometimes, I wouldn't even escape in the night as I'd wake up in a panic. Days would pass, then weeks, then months, and then years. How long? How long must I face this same test? A life of suffering and then what?

And as much as I hated to think of it, a quote came to my mind. A quote I'd heard at Aquinas Catholic College from St. Teresa of Avila, which read, "God, if this is the way You treat Your friends, no wonder You have so few."[2]

I didn't understand when I first heard it, but now the meaning was revealing itself to my soul and my mind. Where my faith and my sight were colliding. Where my friendship with God was looking more like a feud and our love story like a betrayal.

---

[2] Reichardt, Mary R. *Exploring Catholic Literature: A Companion and Resource Guide.* Rowman and Littlefield, 2003. 91.

CHAPTER 7

The weather was warming up and the kids were glad to be able to go outside more often to play. A friend of mine from church, Amy, called to tell me that her children had outgrown their swing set.

"Do you want it?"

"Yes! We'd love to have it."

People were so good to give to us, and I didn't want to miss out on a blessing He put in my path, especially when it came to the kids.

Amy and her husband drove up in their truck and unloaded a wooden swing set—the kids were ecstatic! Michael and his friend worked all afternoon getting it into the ground, hammering the slide to the posts and getting new swings. At the end of the day, we were outside having dinner on our picnic table and watching the kids enjoy our new gift.

As I looked over our white picket fence, I thought back to one of my funniest memories of my early days in Pulaski.

My mom and one of her friends, Linda, had come into town to help me move in and decorate the house. At the time, we had a little dog named Briley. Because we had a weekly trash pick-up, Michael and I would hide our trash bin behind bushes on the side of our house, and roll it out every Wednesday morning before the garbage man arrived.

Linda, mom, and I had done a lot of cleaning and had thrown out a lot of trash. It was early in the morning, and I had not even gotten out of my pajamas, which happened to be a t-shirt and my underwear.

I glanced out the breakfast room window and saw something covering the ground.

Walking toward the window to get a closer look, I saw tons of trash all over the ground! Briley was as happy as he could be, wagging his tail, licking cans of food, and pulling toilet paper out all over the grass.

"Ugh! Briley!"

I thought about running upstairs and putting on a pair of shorts but then thought to myself, "No. No one will see me."

Running out the back door, I started quickly putting the trash back into the bin. The white fence was between me and the street and seemed to be a good enough blocker, I thought. Making my way to the fence, I turned around quickly, reached down, with my bottom in the air and aimed toward the street, and picked up one last piece. Right before I was about to come back up I heard,

"Hey, Rachel!"

I jerked up as quickly as possible to see two of Pulaski's prettiest ladies taking their morning walk.

"Good morning! How are y'all?" I scrambled to pull my t-shirt down over my underwear.

"Good. You okay?" She tugged on her dog's leash.

"Picking up the dog's trash."

I waved and they continued their walk.

I was so embarrassed. I looked at Briley.

"Stupid dog. You're going to cost me my reputation in this town."

Throwing the bags back into the bin, I ran inside the house.

Laughing to myself, thinking how much my life had changed since those days, we watched the kids play until sunset, and I thanked God for a good day.

The summer passed quickly as Michael and I continued to try to book author visits for me and shows for him. Michael was particularly frustrated as the days of calling were turning up nothing. It was a new level of frustration for him. Never had we experienced anything like this.

"I think this is my sign. This is the end. This is where I completely stop performing altogether," he said.

"Really?"

"Yeah. It's ridiculous."

Our baby was upstairs taking a nap, and the kids were having a quiet time. Sitting down in the living room, I thought about all the contacts I'd made—agents, publishers, schools, and festivals. Thinking about it more only convinced me further—I, too, was finished. Thumbing through my years of journaling and realizing how many closed doors we had encountered— I felt a sense of finality flow through me, as well.

"That's it. I'm done."

The baby woke up, and the kids came back downstairs. Michael was on the couch looking through e-mails when I walked in and asked, "Do you mean it? Are you done performing?"

"Yep, I mean it."

"You know what? Me, too. I'm done. I'm done trying to get my stuff off the ground. It's like the Bible verse, 'unless the Lord builds the house, the builders labor in vain.' (Psalm 127:1, NIV). Unless God builds this, our efforts are in vain," I said.

"If God wanted to make this happen, He could do it. But it's not happening, so I'm gonna stop trying."

At that moment, I had an overwhelming desire to do what we were saying. Make a physical representation of it. I walked into our kitchen and took one of Michael's brochures. I grabbed one of each of my books and walked back into the living room.

"Alright, you mean it?" I asked as I held our products in my hands.

"Yes, I do."

"Okay, then let's bury them!" I exclaimed. "Let's bury them, because it's dead as far as I'm concerned."

Michael looked at me.

"Sure, let's bury it. It's dead anyway."

The kids gathered around us.

"What're you doing?" Caroline asked.

"Burying our gifts and talents," I said as if it were completely normal.

Michael stood up. I had the products in one hand and the baby on my hip.

"Let's go," agreed Michael.

We all walked out into the back yard, and Michael picked up a shovel.

"Right about here," he said as he walked over to the swing set.

"Great," I agreed.

He took the shovel and dug a hole. I placed all that was in my hands into the dirt, and Michael covered it back up.

"There," he said, "It's buried."

"Good."

We walked back into the house.

"Let's pray," Michael said as he took my hand.

We all gathered in a circle and held hands as Michael prayed. He asked God to bless us, to protect us, and to put us in the center of His will.

"And, God, we'd love to use our gifts for You, but if that's not Your desire, then we're okay with that. We're letting go of all of it. Lead us and guide us, Lord."

As we stood in a circle, I held the baby and Michael's hand, and I listened carefully to what he was saying. I was glad that we were done with all that caused so much heartache and grief for our family. But I was mourning, too. Mourning the surrender of a dream. The yield of a calling. The resignation of a gift. And as I began to cry for the loss, I heard the Lord clearly say,

"This is a baptism, not a death."

CHAPTER 8

What I was learning in that time of joblessness was people were usually giving us advice. While it seemed well-intentioned, sometimes I got tired of hearing it. I knew we needed a steady income. I knew we needed insurance. I knew we had four kids who needed money for clothes, cars, and college. I knew all of that.

I was tired of hearing other people tell me what I already knew.

And in that time, God began to show me what He looked like as Defender. Before, when I'd read, "I love you, Lord, my strength. The Lord is my rock, my fortress and my deliverer; my God is my rock, in whom I take refuge, my shield and the horn of my salvation, my stronghold," (Psalm 18:1-2, NIV). I liked it, but I had not experienced it.

Now, I was experiencing it.

"God, You are my Defender."

When I could no longer defend myself, and I couldn't, when I could no longer make people understand why we had made the choices we'd made, and I couldn't, God could. "When I can't, God, You can."

It was an awesome thing for me to discover. I got to the point where, when people would give me advice, I would smile and thank them, knowing I did not have to take their advice, nor did I have to give an explanation about the choices Michael and I made.

Not giving an explanation was freeing. How many times had I found myself explaining our actions, defending our decisions, or trying to make other people support what we were doing? How many times? A million, at least. Because, honestly, our lives were looking pretty stupid. But, that was not how it was, at least not with my God. God was giving us our marching orders, and they looked crazy to everyone else. And that was okay. I was learning how to live a life pleasing to God, not to man. And it was freeing indeed.

After Michael came home from the factory, one night, the kids were in bed, and we had our usual "what should we do with our life" conversation.

"I don't understand why we've been led down this road," I said. "We stepped out in faith, away from everything that was safe for us, and have encountered hurdle after trial after crisis. It's been relentless."

"Yeah, you're right. I don't know. Sometimes I feel that I have taken my eyes off of Christ and His plan and placed my eyes strictly on the money," Michael said.

"So, how do we do it?" I asked, "We have to have an income for our family. But, you're right, it's like I don't even want to mess with it. I want to do what God has called us to do and forget about it."

"I don't know. It's like I make money the focus because we need it. But, I have to put my focus on Him."

We sat a moment in silence.

55

"You know there was a time in college when God rescued me. You know when I was dating that guy I thought I might marry. But my family wasn't happy, and truthfully, I didn't have a peace about it. I was desperate. I didn't know what to do. I asked God to rescue me," I paused, "And He did. He can do that again. I'm praying He will."

"Yeah, we've made a decision to follow Christ, and we're gonna do that, no matter what it looks like. No matter where it leads us."

We had committed our path to Him. No matter what it looked like to other people or where He would take us. We had decided to follow Him. Follow Him if He came in and rescued us or follow Him even if He didn't.

"Remember that song I love, 'Burn Us Up?'" I asked Michael as he folded his hands and placed them across his chest.

It was a song I loved about Shadrach, Meshach and Abednego—about them being thrown into the fire. It said, "You have made us, come and save us, we are yours," but the lyric that always stood out to me was, "but even if You don't, we will burn..."[3]

"They said that even if God didn't save them from the fire, they'd obey."

"True," he paused, "but He did."

Days later I was telling a friend about the termite man and what led to our surrender of what we could do in our own strength, and she said, "At this point you'd do anything."

---

[3] Shane & Shane. "Burn Us Up." *Pages.* Inpop Records, 2007.

"Yes, anything. I'm so broken; honestly…whatever, wherever…we would do it!"

"Like, if God asked you to go to Africa to work in an orphanage, you would do it?"

"For sure, we would—we would go," I agreed, "Yes, we would go anywhere, do anything, whatever God wants us to do."

That evening after the kids were in bed, I was laying on the couch thinking of the conversation. Michael came out of our bedroom and was standing at our door, at the foot of the couch, holding his toothbrush.

"You know," I paused, "Jill said something very interesting today that took me off guard, made me stop and think."

"What's that?"

"I was telling her how broken we were, that we were at the bottom, and that we would do whatever God told us to do, no matter what. She laughed and said, 'You'd go to Africa and work in an orphanage if He asked you to, wouldn't you?' I told her we would."

He looked at me as silence filled the air.

Then, very intently, he said, "We should go get on a cruise ship."

At that moment, I felt like I'd never felt before. It was a supernatural awakening. It was a Holy Spirit rush through my body. Words of life to a lifeless body.

I sat up.

"What did you say?" I asked, my eyes gazing into his, my entire body revived with a word.

"What?" he asked, "A cruise ship. We should all go live on a cruise ship."

"A cruise ship," I stopped, feeling like my body had woken up from a very, very deep sleep, "That's it."

"A cruise ship? You think that's it?"

Silence.

"Yes, that's it. That's the answer to our prayers. That's the raft," I paused as I envisioned a cruise ship in my mind. "That's the God-sized raft I've been praying for for over a year."

The Spirit of God overwhelmed me in that moment. An infiltrating feeling of hope in a hopeless body overcame me. My mind raced to the vision God had given me a year prior. The vision of Michael desperately treading in the water when a raft came along and scooped him up. A raft I'd prayed for. A raft I had spent countless hours asking God to send, not knowing what it was, but knowing it was our help in a helpless situation.

A raft that had now arrived in the form of a cruise ship.

CHAPTER 9

We agreed to surrender and let go of what we could do in our human strength. But we also agreed that if the Lord brought us something, we'd gladly accept it. After our conversation about cruise ships, Michael told me he had a friend, Keith, who hired entertainers for the Italian cruise line Costa Concierge. He e-mailed Keith his resume, and we waited.

Several days passed, so Michael spent his days applying for other jobs.

"Anything new today?" I asked one night hoping to hear that he'd gotten a response about the ship.

"Nope, nothing."

We'd finished putting the kids to bed and turned on the TV.

"Good evening, America. Today is September 17, and this is the *Nightly News*."

The music played and the cameras turned to the news anchor.

Our evening ritual—news, then re-runs of *The Office*—was one of my favorite times of the day. Time with just Michael and me—it was a relief to laugh at the characters in the evolving office politics, and it was a temporary escape from our reality.

I looked at Michael lying on the floor. He looked so tired. He was spent.

"He's such a good man," I thought as my heart ached with sorrow for him. It ached for the downward spiral that had brought him so low that I wanted to lower down a rope to help, only I was there with him too. The only small bandage wrapped around my heart on this night was in the form of a thirty-minute situation comedy on the screen on my mantle.

"Tonight we are following a story that has been developing over eighteen months. We turn now to our correspondent, Josh Elliot."

He began, "The stunning feat of engineering overnight. You see the *Costa Concordia*. The cruise ship that capsized. Affixed to a reef there. Lifted from its watery grave and giving us a new view of the immense damage."

My ears perked up.

"What did he say? Did he say what I think he did?"

His words filled the room. His report echoed off the walls.

I squinted to get a closer look. My eyes fixated on the TV.

The *Costa Concordia*. Submerged. Tilted over in the water. Wrecked. Submerged for twenty months, now being lifted out of the water. Today. This day—of all days.

It was being lifted out of the water in slow motion.

I seemed to also be in slow motion as I lifted myself up off the armrest and into an upright position.

"Is this happening? Is that ship being resurrected?"

Watery grave.

The words rang in my ears.

My mother had always described baptism as a watery grave. Death to your old self. Alive, once more, in Christ.

"A watery grave, Rachel." My mind flashed back to a time when my mom was telling me how she described baptism to a young lady she had led to the Lord.

I felt like I had been submerged. For years.

Then the reporter continued, "Lama Hasan is there to show how engineers did it all."

"Good morning, Josh," she said. "It took nineteen long hours, seven hours longer than expected, because they needed to use more pulling force, but they were finally able to pull off this amazing feat. All of it was captured on camera in a stunning time-lapse video. After a long day of pulling and rotating the vessel, maneuvering it so it slowly inches its way up and out of the water, the engineers were able to lift the vessel out of the Mediterranean waters. Celebrations rang out as the most complicated salvage operation in maritime history is now 80% complete. Everyone was pleased, but it's not over yet. You can see the side of the ship covered in slime and scum, where it's been under water for the last twenty months and crushed like a building in an earthquake. Pulling this ship more than twice the size of the *Titanic* was an epic effort."[4]

---

[4] Hasan, Lama. "Costa Concordia Set Upright off Italian Coast." *ABC Nightly News*. ABC News. 17 September 2013. Transcript.

I was now sitting upright on the couch, my eyes not moving one bit. My whole body was like a statue. The words fell on my ears with a THUD.

Then, so clearly, the Lord said to me, *"Just like this ship is being pulled up out of the water, so I am going to pull you up out of the water."*

"Michael, can you believe this?"

The *Costa Concordia* was lifted from its watery grave the exact same week that God delivered my raft in the form of a cruise ship. Not just any cruise line, but the same cruise line that was resurrecting a ship, twenty months after submersion.

"God, you're going to do it. Oh, God. You are going to pull me up out of this watery grave."

And as I watched the news clip in slow motion and listened to the news anchors talking about how a feat like this had never been done before, I knew my resurrection was coming. That although I had felt God had forgotten about me, He hadn't. As sure as this ship was being lifted up out of the water, so He would lift me up out from a watery grave.

CHAPTER 10

The next day, I asked Michael if we could all go as a family to the Episcopal Church to pray. The ornate, historical church sat next to the college that brought us to Pulaski. With doors that were never locked, the church was a place of solitude where Michael and I had gone before to get alone with God and to pray.

"What are we gonna do?" the kids asked as we got into our car.

"Pray," I replied.

We went in, and I passed the pews and went straight up to the altar.

"Come on kids, let's get as close to Jesus as we can."

Putting my face down on the red carpet, alongside Michael and the kids, I held the baby while I reached and touched the edge of the altar. I thought about the woman in the Bible who had bled for twelve years (Luke 8:43-48).

"If only I could touch the hem of his garment..." she thought to herself.

"If only I could touch the hem of Your garment," I said as I rubbed the wood with my hand, "You would heal me."

63

We all said a prayer, even Camille, who was four at the time, and then we sat in the pews in silence.

"God's doing an amazing work, I know He is," I whispered to Michael.

As I was praying, the Lord whispered to my heart,

"You're the messenger. I want you to share your story."

I tucked those words in the back of my mind.

The next day there was no work for Michael at the factory, so he was home. I got up and got the kids dressed while Michael cooked breakfast.

"While you're at Bible study today, I'm going to make calls," he said to me.

"Sounds good."

"I'm telling you we have no money. None," he explained. "Now I don't even have the factory to go to today. We cannot spend a dime."

"That's fine; He's coming through for us," I said as I placed my hands around his waist.

"Well, if He's gonna do that, He needs to do it soon, because I don't have anything left. I'll do anything, you know," he cried as he raised his voice, "Anything. I have bills to pay this week. I'll have to put them on the credit card. I'm so tired of it. If He doesn't have a plan for me, He needs to go ahead and take me."

"Now come on, you know He does. Don't say that; don't get depressed. Come on, you can't do that. He's here with us."

I said it with seriousness—not in a fun or romantic way but in a way I would if I were talking someone off a ledge. It was the conversation we had had for years, but we vacillated between who was on the ledge and who was doing the coercing.

"I love you. We have each other. We have our family. What is the worst case scenario? We lose our house and end up homeless. So what? We have family that would take us in. But we're all still in perfect health. Okay? So if that is the worst thing that could happen, we'd still be okay. Right?"

Silence.

"Right? Come on. If that is the worst thing that happens, who cares? Actually, if we lose everything and starve to death, guess what? We end up in heaven. Come on, that's what Paul says, 'For to me, to live is Christ and to die is gain' (Philippians 1:21, NIV). So if we lose everything and starve, we end up in heaven. So there," I said. "Right? Right, babe?"

"Yeah, you're right. Worst case scenario, we end up in heaven," he chuckled.

"So, you okay?"

"Yeah, I guess."

"I love you." I kissed him, and we held each other. "I'm going to Bible study with the kids, so you'll have the house free to make calls."

As I sat with my Bible open in class, my mind wandered. It seemed crazy to me how back and forth Michael and I were. One day he thought God would not rescue us, the next day I did. I was thankful that God created marriage and knew that he kept us together to console each other when it looked hopeless. I felt sorry for Michael. I thought about what

65

God had shown me in my prayers for a raft and the *Costa* resurrection, but I couldn't convince Michael of these things when he saw a negative bank balance and five faces around the table.

I tuned back into the lesson.

"I loved what Brother Tony said this past Sunday," our Bible study teacher stated.

Then she looked right at me and asked, "When's the last time you've asked God for a miracle?"

It sent a chill down my spine.

"Lord, You know I've asked You over and over for a miracle. But, I'm asking again—give my family a miracle," I prayed.

When I arrived home, Michael was sitting on the floor with his Bible open. He looked like he'd been crying.

"I've been crying out to God. Literally crying out to Him. Crying my eyes out and begging Him to stop it, begging Him to stop what He's doing to my family."

"He's going to, okay? He will."

We sat there on the floor and held each other.

"I've been sitting here, crying my eyes out to God. Yelling and crying, asking Him to show me His purpose for me or to take me away," he said.

"He's showing you. He's answering your prayers. As you are crying out to Him, He's answering!" I said, "He's doing it. He's sending the raft. He's going to rescue our family. He already has, okay? Let's start thanking Him for it."

We sat there, holding each other.

"I made a ton of calls, and no one, I mean not one person, was interested. I was so frustrated that I'm sitting here right now with no money and looking at y'all's picture," he pointed to our family photo from Texas, "with no way to take care of y'all," he started to cry, "so I cried out to God to help me."

"And He is. He's going to do it."

We held each other a few more minutes when Michael got a call. He answered, talked a few minutes then said as he hung up, "Good, the factory asked me to come in."

"Great!"

"It's a Band-Aid. I'm thankful, but I need something that'll support my family."

"God will do it. He will. He's making a way."

After Michael left, I made the kids lunch, and as we were sitting down at the table, my phone rang.

"Hey!" I said as I answered, looking at the number.

"Guess what?" Michael asked, sounding excited.

"What?"

"Guess who I just got off the phone with?"

"Who?"

"Keith Cox!"

"Thank God! What did he say?"

"He wants me to come on the *Costa Luminosa* in December, Baby!"

"Yes! I knew it!"

He said Costa would fly him from Nashville to Miami, where Michael would board the boat, and then he'd perform two or three shows within ten days. They would then fly him from the island, where they would be docked, back to Nashville. He would have two weeks off, and then he would be out again for ten days. He would do this from December until April.

My heart was overflowing with joy for the miracles I'd seen play out in front of my eyes. God was delivering an answer to years of our prayers within a few hours. I didn't know how it would all work out. All I knew was that God seemed to be in every detail of it.

CHAPTER 11

After he came back from his last cruise of the season, he was renewed and seemed happy that God had clearly spoken to him. He had talked to the cruise line about possibly working for them in Italy, but when that didn't work out, he asked God for continued direction.

"I told God if He wanted me to use my talents, He had to send me help. We both know that I can't do this without help. I've asked for years for God to send me someone who can promote the show and help with the marketing."

"Yeah, that's right. We both know you can't do it alone."

"And, you know, God gave me a vision of Dane Moore. Remember him?"

"Kinda. Who is he again?"

"He was one of the guys in charge of the shows in Cabot, Arkansas. Remember? We performed there twice."

"Okay, yeah, I remember. So why do you think God gave you a vision of Dane?"

"Well, I think he'd be a great promoter. He's always liked the show, and I think he might have what it takes to help me."

Several days later, as I was coming down the stairs with my laundry basket in my hands, I looked at my bridal portrait on the wall as I had done so many times before. No sooner had I reached the bottom of the stairs, I saw a vivid vision:

A broken and shattered vase, tiny fragments, all over the place.

Then I heard,

"Unless you become like that..."

I sat down on the couch in my parlor.

Then again,

"Unless you become like that..."

Instantly, I knew. Unless I became broken and poured out for others to see, hear, and read about, there was no fragrance released to the room. As long as I was all put together, withholding the perfume, no one could enjoy it. But if I would become broken, it would release incense that would invite many over to see and marvel in the Lord's works.

I surrendered.

"All right, Lord, that's it. I'll break open for all to see what You've done for me. I'll tell whatever You want me to. Give me an audience. Show me how to share my story."

I spoke with a friend who had done some work for us about creating a blog for me. After she quoted me a price, I knew our money was too tight for me to afford it, so I told her through a text that I'd have to wait on it. Several hours later, she sent me a response—the Lord had told her to do it for me for free.

Holding my notes in my hand as I sat in my rocking chair, tears began to fall from my face.

"What do you want your domain name to be?" she asked.

"Rachel's Raft," I said as I was standing in faith of all God had done, "Yes, that's what I want to name it."

My blog posts were forthright from the beginning: I came out swinging. I wanted to unleash the work that God was doing, so I decided to become that broken vase. Several hundred people began following my blog, encouraging me to continue to write and thanking me for being open about our struggles, so I kept writing.

In the meantime, Michael called Dane Moore and told him his story from the ship, and Dane agreed to pray for us and to partner with Michael, however he could, to help him market his show.

We agreed to let God move in His time, to let Him take the next step, and when people asked us about it, we said, "What are we going to do? Nothing. We're doing nothing. We're trusting God to deliver us and waiting for Him to do it."

I felt strongly about my answer. I read the story of the parting of the Red Sea (Exodus 14) and realized how God received all the glory because there was nothing in the Israelites' power that could have caused an escape like that.

While Michael was working at the factory, I prayed and believed for a supernatural deliverance.

Towards the end of May, we vacillated from trusting to worrying. Michael had been back at the factory for three months with no other job opportunities in sight, and I wondered why

God had shown me the resurrection of the cruise ship? Why the termite man? What about what He had said about pulling me up out of the water? Michael would wake up and face another day; as would I. I thought about what people had asked. I didn't know how we would make it or how we would ever climb out of our growing debt.

One night, I got into bed thankful that I could sleep and not think about what was going to happen to me or my family, and I was reminded of a conversation I'd had with my friend, Abigail, the previous year. I'd called her for prayer for our family, and several weeks later she called me, "Rachel, you're going to think this is crazy..."

"No, I promise I won't," I assured her.

"Well, okay. This morning during praise and worship at our church, I was praying for you and Michael, and God gave me a vision of an anchor. Rachel, God's not going to leave you flailing around at sea. He is your anchor."

My mind immediately thought of the verse in Hebrews, "This hope we have as an anchor of the soul, a *hope* both sure and steadfast and one which enters within the veil" (Hebrews 6:19, NASB). I didn't know whether to laugh or to cry. It was so personal. So as I lay in bed that night, I wanted to totally trust Him, but it was so hard. I couldn't see what He was doing.

"My anchor holds within the veil..." I said to myself. "God, I don't have a clue what You are up to. I thought we'd be living in Italy, and here we are in Pulaski. I thought You'd freed us. Where is this resurrection You promised me?"

I couldn't see it.

So I waited, hoping He would deliver on His word.

We continued to pray, fast, and wait.

Summer arrived, and we continued to wait. One Sunday evening we were at our neighbor's house swimming when Michael received a text from Dane:

Please call me, on speaker with Rachel, as soon as you get this.

"What do you think it is? Do you think it's good news?" I asked Michael.

"I don't know. Hopefully."

We got the kids out of the pool, dried them off, and drove home. After we'd bathed them and gotten them in bed, we called Dane and Heather.

"Hey, how's it going?" Michael asked.

"Good," they said on speakerphone.

"Well, we wanted to talk to you guys about something," Dane continued. "Heather's parents live in a small, tourist town in the Ozarks called Mountain View."

"We've been there before. I had a show north of that town, and everyone told us to visit there," Michael said.

"So you know what I'm talking about? Well, we got back from visiting her mom and dad, and we drove past a theater, like a live entertainment theater, and it's up for rent. So, we asked around and found out that the former entertainer owned a store on the square. We went to talk to her, and she told us all about the theater. She'd been there thirty years and had decided to retire, and now it's up for rent."

Pause.

73

"So, we were wondering if maybe this is an open door from the Lord. We've already planned to move to Mountain View at some point, and I've always wanted to own something like that," Dane continued.

"So, you want to own a theater and maybe have Michael as your entertainer?" I questioned, my heart skipping a beat.

"Yes, that's what we're thinking about. Maybe this is the reason I came to your mind when you were praying on the ship," Dane said.

Michael and I stared at each other in disbelief.

We continued to speak with them about what all it would involve. Michael had always liked the idea of entertaining in a theater, so we continued to talk about the logistics—the seating, location, brainstorming ideas for promotion, all sorts of things, when I felt compelled to say, "The only thing that's keeping us in Pulaski is our house. So if we get an offer on the house tomorrow after being on the market for three years, we'll know it's God's will."

We talked another half an hour, and I said it again, two more times. I felt compelled to do so. Being a part of a theater had always been a dream of Michael's, and we'd been waiting on God to open a door; perhaps this was it.

After we hung up, Michael and I spent the rest of the evening, even into the early hours of the morning, exchanging ideas and thinking up new plans for what might be the very sea God was parting. We agreed that the house was the only thing keeping us in Pulaski, and if God would sell it, we would be free to go wherever.

CHAPTER 12

The next morning when the phone rang, I was not surprised to hear the realtor on the other end. We'd waited years for God to move us and believed this was it. She wanted to show the house, so I cleaned like crazy. The showing was at 2:00 p.m., and I used every minute from the time she called until 1:59 to make it presentable. An hour later, I figured they must have loved it. An hour after that, the realtor called with an offer on our house!

"Hallelujah! Thank you, Jesus! You are making all things new (Revelation 21:5)!"

We were so excited! We were ecstatic!

The next several days involved the inspector coming, the termite inspection, and the appraisal. We were set to close on my birthday, July 25th.

"What an awesome birthday gift that will be," I stated.

"Don't pack yet," our realtor said. "Don't pack until it all goes through."

But we'd already waited two weeks. With the closing was only two weeks away, we started packing the house. The buyers came by to visit, and they were as excited as we were. I thought it was a done deal.

Dane and Heather wanted us to come to Mountain View for a visit to check out the theater and find a house of our own. We wanted to rent a house until we knew exactly where we wanted to live in Mountain View, so I started looking online and found a rental home. We planned on signing the lease for the theater, signing a lease for the rental home, and exploring our new surroundings. We'd spent so much time in prayer for so many months. We had a peace about everything that was coming forth.

We took the kids to Michael's parents for the weekend and headed towards Arkansas. After stopping in Memphis to eat lunch, we had just gotten back on the highway when my phone rang.

"Hello?" I said as I put it on speaker.

"Rachel, this is Susan. Listen, I have some bad news."

My heart dropped to the floor.

"The couple is withdrawing their offer."

Silence.

"What?"

"The couple has decided to withdraw their offer. I know this is terrible news."

"What do you mean they're withdrawing their offer?"

"Well, because it's a VA loan and because there were some issues with the inspection, they've decided to go with a different house."

I looked over at Michael whose color was draining from his face.

"Can they do that, I mean legally? Susan, we're supposed to close one week from today!"

"Well, yes, they can. I mean, you can sue if you want to."

"We don't want to do that. But I don't know how they can bail when we are one week from closing the house!"

"Well, I know it's awful, but there's nothing we can do. I've seen closings fall apart on the day of closing. It's terrible for y'all, but there's nothin' we can do about it."

"Okay," I agreed as my voice trembled. "Thanks for calling. We'll talk to you later."

Michael was in shock. He looked at me and seemed frightened.

"You've got to be kidding me," he stammered.

"Nope, they bailed," I cried in disgust.

"How can they do that? We're supposed to close one week from today,"

"I know. I have no idea."

We were hours away from signing the papers on our new life. My heart sank thinking about what our next step would be. I wondered if I'd ever heard from God. It seemed like things were always close to working out but never actually did. God seemed like He was always about to work in our favor, and then He'd pull the plug. Did I even know Him? Did I ever hear His voice?

We continued to drive in silence having no idea what we would do once we arrived in Mountain View.

I knew Michael was as mad and upset as I was. He thought we were definitely in God's will, but then it all changed.

When we finally pulled into town, we sat across the street from where we were supposed to meet Dane and Heather. We talked about leaving and going back to Nashville to get the kids. Then we talked about telling Dane and Heather we would not be moving to Arkansas. Finally, we decided to pray. Afterwards, we decided to meet with them and not to say anything about the house yet. We were so confused and didn't want to make any decisions about anything.

I put on my best smile and tried to be as pleasant as I possibly could. I was not at all hungry but tried to act like I was. We made a lot of small talk; then they took us on a tour: the sparkling White River, the town square complete with live music, a fudge shop, restaurants, and, of course, the theater that we thought we'd be a part of but now seemed out of reach. After the tour, we went back to the small apartment we'd rented for the night and agreed to meet Dane and Heather in the morning for breakfast.

Michael and I decided to take a walk around the square which was across the street from where we were staying. We talked about all the different scenarios, but the one that seemed the most realistic was the one that involved not having two mortgages. There was no way around it. So, we decided that in the morning we would tell Dane and Heather that we could not be a part of the theater. We were devastated.

As we walked down Main street, we passed a clothing store.

"Look!" Michael exclaimed as he pointed to a t-shirt hanging in the window.

I glanced up and saw an anchor. As if it were hanging there specifically for me.

On it was written, "This hope we have as an anchor of the soul, a hope both sure and steadfast and one which enters within the veil...Hebrews 6:19" (NASB).

We took our picture in front of it so that I could remember the trip to Mountain View and reflect on the verse that had challenged my faith while holding me steadfast to His promises.

At 1:39 a.m., I woke up with knots in my stomach. I turned the corner to go into the living area. Michael was also awake, praying. I sat down on the other chair, picked up my Bible, and numbly read whatever I could find. Nothing was sinking in. I might as well have been reading a *Southern Living* magazine as I could not process any verses or their truths. We sat there and talked, prayed, and cried until 4:00 in the morning.

The next morning, we walked to the square and were the first people at the coffee shop. The barista was putting on his apron as we sat down, ordered coffee, and told him our entire story. He was a Christian and encouraged us with his own life story and how God had worked with him in broken circumstances. We continued from there and met with the owner of the rental home. She was excited and hoped that we would come and entertain in the beloved Mountain View theater. She drove us up Dodd Mountain to her cabin on the hill. The view was breathtaking as we saw the entire town as well as the Ozarks that bordered it. We stayed for an hour and looked, but in our hearts, we didn't think it would be a home to us.

After we left, we drove to meet Dane and Heather, and when we did, Michael told them that up until the day before, we were all in, but then there was a turn of events. He told them our house had not sold and that we were not certain of anything anymore. The tears started to fall down my face and onto my salad plate. Then, I put my head down on the table.

When I brought it back up, I cried, "I'm broken. That's all I can say. Broken."

All was quiet.

"You guys take a week. Think it over. Pray about it. We're not going anywhere. Let's see what the Lord wants us to do," they told us. And with that, Heather reached into her purse and handed me a gift.

Then the tears started to flow steadily. It was like it was a present sent straight from my Father's hands: a paperweight with an engraving of a promise. Here He was again, reassuring me that in spite of the waves that seemed to overtake me, He was sending the raft.

"Heather," I explained with dewy eyes, "if you only knew how much this means to me," my voice trembled as I reached over and hugged her tightly.

We drove home in silence and spent the next week doing nothing. Not packing. Not unpacking. But sitting, praying, reading, and listening. One verse I read struck me as it became my own prayer:

"Deliver me from the mire and do not let me sink; May I be delivered from my foes and from the deep waters. May the flood of water not overflow me Nor the deep swallow me up, Nor the pit shut its mouth on me" (Psalm 69:14, NASB).

My mom had called to tell me that while she was in church, she felt the Lord telling her to pay for our first four months of rent in Mountain View. She spoke with my dad about it, and they agreed to help us out financially.

"We want to help y'all out. If you don't go, you'll always wonder what would've been. So, think about it. If y'all decide to move, we can help you the first few months," she suggested. We were so grateful for the offer and agreed to continue to pray.

CHAPTER 13

My birthday arrived, and Michael and was going to take me out on a date. We'd talked throughout the week as to the decision we were going to make. Dane and Heather needed an answer and had asked us to give them one within the week. They were ready and willing to sign the lease for the theater but needed to know our plans first. My heart started changing for Mountain View, and I no longer wanted to go as the circumstances had shifted.

With the kids gone and Michael and I about to go on our date, we got down on our faces in the living room and prayed again for clarity.

"Lord, we thought you wanted us in Mountain View, but when the buyers backed out, we were confused. Please show us what you want us to do."

I was brushing my hair and putting on make-up before we left when he came in, "You are not gonna believe the news clip I just watched."

"What? What was it?" I asked numbly.

"No, I'm not going to tell you. I want you to come see it."

I set down my brush and walked into the living room as Michael stood by the television set with the remote for the TV in his hands. He clicked the NBC news icon as I stared at the screen:

I stood there—stunned. In silence, I watched a clip of the *Costa Concordia*, once again in the news.

She was on a four day journey to the port where she began her journey nine years previously. She was being pulled by tugboats to the port in Genoa, Italy where she would be broken apart and used for scrap for boats all over the world. It was the first time she'd moved since her resurrection in September of the previous year.[5] And as I watched her being pulled, I couldn't help but think how she looked like she was being tugged against her will.

"I bet you can't believe this, can you?" Michael asked.

"No, I can't," I said as I stared at the images on the screen.

"I need some time to pray," I stated in amazement while thinking of how God was using this ship again in my life.

Michael left the room, and with my face on the floor in the silence and stillness, I heard,

"Your will. Surrendered."

---

[5] Jameson, Alastair. "Costa Concordia Cruise Liner Towed in Final Voyage from Giglio." 23 July 2014. *NBC News*. www.nbcnews.com.

It was like a pendulum that had been swinging back and forth was now coming into direct alignment with its central position.

"Okay, Lord, I surrender. I'll go wherever; do whatever. I've said it, and I mean it."

I knew I had to surrender. And if this was what God had in mind, then I would follow.

"If you want me to go to Mountain View, Lord, I'll go. Even though it doesn't make sense and even though I don't know how it'll all work, I'll go."

Throughout the evening, Michael and I discussed how God would work it all out. We agreed—moving was the next step for us to take.

The days that followed involved packing up what we would need for the next several months. We didn't need everything we owned because the house we were renting was furnished and our house in Pulaski would remain on the market.

The day before we left for Arkansas, I was reading in Psalms 34. Many verses jumped out at me, but these spoke to me the most:

"This poor man cried, and the Lord heard him And saved him out of all his troubles. The angel of the Lord encamps around those who fear Him And rescues them" (Psalms 34:6-7, NASB).

I circled the word "rescues" (v. 7).

Then I went on to read:

"The *righteous* cry, and the Lord hears And delivers them out of all their troubles" (Psalms 34:17, NASB).

I circled the word "all" (v. 17).

Then I read:

"Many are the afflictions of the righteous, But the Lord delivers him out of them all" (Psalms 34:19).

I circled the word "all" (v. 19).

"God, I pray that You would rescue us. I pray that You would help Michael. Set him free. Use him in the way You want to. Give him success and help him to provide for us.

It was normal for me to pray for Michael and to ask for favor and for the Lord to bless his shows and all his work. But this time I heard something that took me by surprise:

"It's you I'm resurrecting."

"What, Lord?"

"It's you I'm resurrecting."

"It's me?" I wondered.

But it was such a clear answer and a thought I'd never had, so I knew it was from God. It was the way He spoke to me—it was clear, out of the ordinary, and it gave me a lot of peace and joy!

"It's me You're resurrecting? Okay, Lord. I'm ready."

I felt prompted to pray for a spiritual time out for Michael. I'd seen him work harder in the past seven years than ever, and I thought he was in great need of a season of rest somehow. I longed for a season where he would be still and quiet and not have to work his fingers to the bone. I trusted the income from the theater would be a blessing and a guarantee of work that he would not have to solicit, but we knew he would need to do something on the side to help cover all our expenses.

As we packed up our U-Haul that day, I was confident in the new adventure, knowing God was taking us to the Ozarks.

When we arrived, we unpacked, and five days later I wrote in my journal:

I think I'm going to write a book, *Rachel's Raft.*

I enjoyed writing the blog, but all of a sudden, I had an overwhelming desire to get the entire story out in a memoir. It was like I couldn't tell the stories fast enough—like I'd been held under water for a very long time, and our move to Mountain View was my first breath since immersion.

Michael and I in his theater in Mountain View, Arkansas

Since arriving in Mountain View, I'd found time to write since Michael was at home during the week while entertaining on the weekends.

"I want to turn 'Rachel's Raft' into a book. What do you think?" I asked.

"Sure! Go for it! It's a great story."

So my time down at the library went from writing posts to starting a memoir. The first day I sat down to write, I knew immediately where I was going to start.

"I'm going to start with the picture of myself that I looked at so often and wondered what I would say to the girl in the bridal portrait...if I could..."

Then I wrote and wrote and wrote. It flowed out of me—there was no stopping it.

And when I prayed abou/t it, the only direction I got was to write it; I needed to trust God with all the rest.

"What will you do when you finish your book?" my mom asked me.

"I have no idea, I know I'm supposed to write it and that God is going to show me what to do with it when I'm done."

"You think you'll find a publisher when you're finished?"

"Yeah, I think so. Actually, I think publishing will be part of the story."

So, I continued to write not having an ending in mind, but never did I imagine what God had in store.

CHAPTER 14

We received a bouquet of crimson roses and a lunch invitation from a local church upon our arrival to Mountain View. Michael had made contact with them before we moved, and we were touched by their thoughtfulness. When the pastor's wife, Karen, and I went to pick up lunch, she asked, "So, tell me a little about yourself. How do you like it here?"

I paused.

"Well, honestly, I feel like I'm coming out of a deep, dark valley I've walked in for about ten years," I said to her as I looked out at the perfectly manicured lawn across the street from the church, so perfect I felt compelled to compliment it. "That's the most beautiful yard I've ever seen," I observed as I placed my purse on my lap and buckled my seatbelt.

"Over there?" she asked pointing to the light blue house. "That's Mr. Grisham's house. He's a member at our church. You know John Grisham?"

"The author?"

"Yes. It's his mom and dad's house."

"Huh, they have a nice yard."

She smiled and turned down the street towards the diner where we were getting our food.

God had worked many things in my life by this point. Being more open to share our struggles was one of those, so turning back to our conversation, I continued, "Three years ago, God gave His Word as a promise: He will make all things new" (Revelation 21:5).

My thoughts took me back to that time, three years ago, when I was sitting in our mechanic's driveway in Pulaski. We had finished a week of traveling and raising money for ministries, and I was out early getting an oil change. My heart was heavy that morning as I sat on a picnic bench, heavy from the financial woes that plagued our family, and as I waited for the minivan to be finished, I looked out at the wheat field across the street. Watching the sun rise and shower the crop with light, I heard in my spirit,

"I make all things new."

It caught me off guard, but it gave me a glimpse of hope. Hope that I had not felt in a long time. And I carried that hope with me. I carried it right up to the top of the mountain where we now lived. And as I reflected on our new view of Ozark beauty, I believed God was delivering on His promise.

As my focus returned to our conversation, I smiled and looked at Karen. "I'm glad to be here."

During our lunch, the minister of the church, Pastor Roger, told us when Michael had originally called, he felt the Lord tell him he should consider Michael for a pastoral position. The shock on our faces might have revealed how stunned we were by a possible position after many years of struggling to find work. Roger told us it would involve a lengthy process, but if we were open to it, they'd love to have us at their church and possibly on their staff. Michael was elated, and I was still in shock.

"Can you believe how hard it was for us to find work in Tennessee, and now you not only have one job, you might have two?" I asked Michael on our way home.

Michael in front of the Costa Luminosa, the ship where he entertained

The theater salary was not enough to support our family, and we knew that when we took the job. We'd found renters for our house in Tennessee but heard they were breaking our rental agreement, so an eviction notice was on its way. The idea of two house payments was overwhelming and something we knew we couldn't afford. Thankfully, Costa asked him to entertain again during the winter months.

Michael knew he would have to have another part-time job of some sort to make ends meet, but when he thought he might have a position at the church, he waited. And as he waited, I continued to write.

One morning, I woke up suddenly with a vivid dream on my mind.

"Whoa, what was that?" I thought as I laid there in bed replaying it. In my dream I was behind a curtain with about twenty five other women. We were all dressed in white robes, and I was laying on a table with my hands folded across my chest.

All the ladies were talking and whispering,

"God's about to do something amazing through someone. Who is it? Who is it?" they were saying as they were turning around looking at the ladies standing around them.

I knew it was me.

Then a whisper rippled through the room…

"It's Rachel Kelley. It's Rachel Kelley."

That's when I suddenly woke up.

"God, it is me, isn't it?"

The first time we attended a Wednesday night church supper, there was a large amount of seating available at the end of one table for our large family. So, I took the kids' trays and drinks and set them down across from, surprisingly enough, Mr. and Mrs. Grisham. Mrs. Grisham lit up as she saw the baby coming to sit down next to her. She oohed and aahed over Mary Manor's every move and watched her as she ran around the fellowship hall opening and closing cabinet doors.

The next week, Michael was already down the hall helping with the children's program when the kids and I sat in our same spot.

"How are you tonight, Mr. Grisham?"

"I'm okay."

"Good," I replied as Mary Manor scooped up a bite of soup and pointed it toward Mr. Grisham.

He smiled from ear to ear.

"No thank you, I've already eaten," he said as he laughed and grinned.

She insisted and pulled out another bite as the vegetables dribbled down her own chin.

"Thank you. That is so nice, but I'm full," he said again as he smiled.

I laughed as well, and my heart warmed thinking about it.

"This is such an interesting turn of events," I thought to myself as I sat for a moment in reflection.

Then later that night, as it was on my mind, I asked Michael, "Do you think it's a coincidence that we could be anywhere in the world, and we're here in Mountain View, Arkansas?"

"No, I don't. What do you think?" Michael asked.

"I don't think there are any coincidences in God's plans."

CHAPTER 15

In late November, the church voted down the motion to hire a family minister. We were assured it had nothing to do with us, only budgetary and personnel commitments that were already in place. We were disappointed, of course, but told the pastor and his wife we had come for the theater and asked them to not feel bad over the decision. Inwardly, we were wondering about provision once again.

Two mornings later Michael received a text from the theater manager about the importance of promoting the show and filling the seats. "Why would God take us to a church just to be turned down for a job?" Michael vented, "And now this! We've got to have more people coming to the theater!"

I was thinking about the job falling through, the double house payments, and the theater manager's message when the phone rang—it was a friend from church. She consoled me, assuring me the congregation was uncomfortable with the process; their decision wasn't personal.

"Honestly it would be okay under normal circumstances, but this has happened to us over and over and over again. I know you don't know much about our lives before we came here, but this is nothing new to us. We've been through years of being led in a direction only to have the doors closed in front of us. And I'm not talking about a little door that lightly shuts, but more like a door that is slammed shut and bolted tight. Sometimes Michael and I feel God is dangling a carrot in front of us, and we chase and chase it, only to find that it's not ours to obtain. It seems unending," I vented.

"Well, Rachel, that's not God. If you think He's dangling stuff in front of you, that's not the way He works. He has a plan for you. I know He does. I know He has something awesome for you and your family."

"I think He does, too, but I'm asking Him to show us. We've had miracles, signs, and wonders, and I know He has a plan, too. But we are so tired and so weary."

"Rachel, I know it must be hard for you to get away by yourself, but if you could get alone with God, you'll find your peace again. That's what I have to do. When I'm feeling like you are right now, I need to get alone with God and find His peace."

"Yeah." I paused. "I know that's what I need right now."

I was even more upset after we'd hung up. It was like I'd had a couple of days for my wound to heal, but now I'd pulled the bandage back off. I wanted to cry. I was about to meet a friend for lunch. I didn't want to have mascara running down my face, but deep down, I wanted a good, soaking cry. I met her and she wanted to know the details of the church vote. So I dug up all the feelings once again and shared them. After our lunch, I was emotionally spent.

I drove down the hill to a small Lutheran church where no cars were parked. I assumed no one was there, but I got out anyway and tried the doors only to find they were locked. I drove further down the road, saw the sign for the Catholic Church, and pulled into the parking lot. Grabbing my purse and my scarf, I got out and walked to the front door.

The lights were on, so I turned down the hallway to see a priest sitting at a table in the conference room. "Hello! How are you?" as he reached out his hand, "Please come sit down," he pointed to the chair next to him, almost as if he were expecting me. "What's your name?"

"I'm Rachel. Are you the pastor here?"

"Yes, I am, Rachel. That's a beautiful Biblical name. I'm glad you've come today."

"Thank you. I was wondering if I could use your sanctuary to pray."

"Certainly. I'll walk you down and turn on the lights." For some reason, his Irish accent comforted me.

There were rosary beads hanging by the sanctuary door with a sign: "Please Take One." I thought of what my mentor, JoAnne, had explained, "I know some Protestants think we Catholics keep Christ on the cross because we talk more about His death than His resurrection, but that's not why. We look at Him on the cross so we can remember His suffering."

"I definitely need to think of His suffering today," I thought as I grabbed one from the hook.

"There you go, Rachel," the priest said as he turned on the lights.

"Thank you. You have kneeling benches, right? I need to get on my knees before God."

I headed to the front pew as he walked out of the sanctuary and pulled down the kneeler. After setting down my purse and taking off my scarf, I took the beads in my hands, got on my knees, and looked at Christ on the cross.

"Jesus, I know you suffered. I can't imagine how much You suffered for me, but God, I'm human, and I can't take much more…" Tears started flowing down my face. "God, please, I can't take it anymore. I am begging, pleading, please, please stop our suffering."

Then the tears came with a vengeance. Before I knew it, I was sobbing. Sobbing so hard the tears soaked my face. They moved from my face to my black leggings and onto the carpet. There was no stopping them. I wept, like I'd never wept before, the kneeler shaking from the depth of my cry.

"I'm begging You to make it stop. God, here I am in a Catholic church, just as I was ten years ago. You placed me on the anvil at Aquinas College, and now here I am in Mountain View ten years later, still being hammered on. I'm begging. I'm pleading for You to make it stop."

The tears were too much now, so I walked to the back of the church and found some tissue. I wiped my face and my pants and sat back down, staring at Him on the cross, as the tears continued to flow.

"Your word says that trials have a time limit (1 Peter 5:10). They can't go on forever, right?" I thought of Psalm 23:4a, "Even though I walk through the valley of the shadow of death, I will fear no evil" (NASB), and prayed that we'd walk through the valley, not sit down and stay there forever. "Bring this to an end." Gazing at Him on the cross, I pleaded, "Look at me. Look at me, Your daughter. I am Your child. I am in need."

I couldn't even think of what else to pray; it was all I could pray: the last question on the test, the final plague of the locusts, the last wave before the calm. I continued to weep for what seemed like a long time when I heard the sanctuary doors open and the shuffle of the priest's feet. They shuffled all the way to the pew directly behind me. Then all I could hear was a whisper of a prayer, perhaps an intercession for me. He walked to the back of the sanctuary and out the door. I wiped my face, my pants, and my hands and tried to regain composure. Then I gathered my belongings and walked out of the sanctuary.

I noticed him sitting in the conference room again. He stood up, took my hands, and said, "Rachel, what is it?"

With my face still damp from the tears, I cried, "My family... I just want God to change our circumstances..." I wiped my face with a tissue.

"May I pray for you?"

He put his hands on my forehead and asked for blessings in the name of the Father, and of the Son, and of the Holy Spirit then squeezed my hands and invited me back anytime I wanted. Getting into the car, I hung the beads on my rearview mirror as a reminder of God's promises for trials to come to an end as I read in 1 Peter 5:10, "And after you have suffered for a little while, the God of all grace, who called you to his eternal glory in Christ, will Himself perfect, confirm, strengthen *and* establish you" (NASB).

The next day was Michael's low. After breakfast and after we talked about the job falling through, the renters leaving, and the theater's season, he excused himself to the bathroom, where I later found him crying.

I sat down next to him. As tears rolled down his face, he asked, "What is God doing? Why does He keep doing this? Why? I want to know! Why does He treat me like this? Why?"

He grabbed the toilet paper roll, pulled several feet from it, and wiped his nose and his eyes.

"I mean, why? I can't take care of y'all like I need to. You need to find someone else."

"No, babe, I don't. We've already talked about this. It's you and me. He told me He would send a raft, and He has."

"Well, it has a hole in it, and it's sinking."

"No, that's not the kind of raft He sends."

As I placed my hands on his back, I continued, "God has a plan. He does."

"I need to sit in here alone."

"Let me pray for you first."

I cupped his hands into mine and prayed God would give Michael peace and show him that God was for us not against us (Romans 8:31), as it sometimes seemed.

CHAPTER 16

One evening, Michael was performing at the theater and the children were with their grandparents for the weekend, so I decided to spend time working on my book at McDonald's. When I arrived at 4:00 p.m., I ordered coffee and began to write. After about four hours, I finished the last chapter—the chapter where we'd left for Mountain View.

"Okay, God, that's 175 pages completed. Now You've got to show me how to end this book."

I packed up my laptop and headed home. I put some soup on the stove to eat for dinner and sat down on the couch. Looking at the clock, I knew I still had an hour before Michael would be home.

"Maybe I'll keep writing." I got on my knees next to the couch and prayed, "Lord, what do You want me to do?"

Clearly I heard,

"Rest."

"Okay," I said as I got up and put away my journals and laptop.

When Michael came home, I told him I'd arrived at my stopping place and that God had to show me how to end the book.

"Yeah, you need a good ending, not a sad one," he laughed.

"Seriously," I said. "When I prayed tonight, the Lord told me to rest, so I'm going to do that until He shows me what to do next. I'm asking Him to show me an ending for *Rachel's Raft*. An awesome one."

The next morning, Michael came to me with an idea.

"Pastor Roger asked me to come to breakfast. I think you need to come, too, and ask him about the Grisham family maybe helping you with your book," he said as he sat down on the bed. "Seriously, you're about done with it. You should at least ask."

The thought had crossed my mind after we'd met his family, but I was not at a place where I wanted to try to "make" it happen. If it was what God wanted, He would open the doors.

"You know what would be amazing? If they opened the door to the conversation without me saying a word," I said as we drove to their house.

"Oh, that would be."

As we sat around the dining room table, we talked about the upcoming Christmas play and the choir that had worked so hard to prepare for the production. Then they asked what we were planning on doing while the kids were gone, and Michael replied, "Well, Rachel had a lot of time to work on her book yesterday."

"Yeah, I wrote for about four hours and am kinda at a stopping place."

"Rachel, that reminds me," Karen chimed in, "I wanted to let you know I ran into Mr. Grisham's daughter last night at Wal-Mart. She's in town for a few days, and I told her about you. I asked her if she'd be willing to look at your children's books sometime."

"Really?"

"She has connections in publishing, and she said she'd be happy to take a look at your stuff."

Michael gently nudged my foot under the table.

"Uh, yeah, uh, that would be awesome. Wow, thanks," I stammered. "Thanks," I said, knowing in my heart it was *Rachel's Raft* that I needed to share with them. "You know as much as I love my children's books, I think they've only paved the way for what I've written in this book, so if I could share this with the Grisham family, that would be awesome."

"I'm sure that'd be fine," she replied.

"You know, that's amazing. I want to tell y'all something. Before we moved here, I felt led to pray for a spiritual time-out for Michael. I didn't even know what it meant or what it looked like, but I knew that it was what I was to pray. So, when we came here and y'all talked to him about possibly working at your church, it put him in a holding pattern."

"So it's not our fault. It might actually be your fault," Karen laughed. We all laughed.

"Yeah, I guess you're right. But in that time, I was able to sit down and start my book like I knew God was leading me to do."

After we left their house, I called my friend Michelle, who'd read every word of my manuscript. She answered, "I've been praying! What happened?" Then she started in again before I could answer the question. "Actually, before you say anything, let me tell you this. When you texted me this morning, I was still asleep, and Rachel, I was having a dream about you. You were releasing chapters of your book at a bookstore, and people were lined up to get them. Rachel, this isn't just any old book that people are going to read and think 'that was nice.' This book is going to have an effect on people's lives."

I continued my work on *Rachel's Raft* as God led, and I felt confident God had His hand on me as the words continued to flow when I would sit down to write. Reflecting on our time in Mountain View and realizing the underlying power which had brought us there made me stand in awe.

I hadn't read any of John Grisham's books since high school, so one afternoon, while the kids were upstairs, I grabbed my phone and sat down on the couch. I typed in the name "John Grisham," and his website came up. Immediately, I noticed his publisher's logo was an

Dinner on our front porch overlooking Mountain View

anchor. Clicking the navigation bar, I scrolled over and chose the Bio link. Moving down the page, I read about his upbringing, college career, his bestselling novels…

I almost closed out the window when I started to read the next paragraph. That's when my finger froze to the screen:

Grisham took time off from writing for several months in 1996 to return, after a five-year hiatus, to the courtroom. He was honoring a commitment made before he had retired from the law to become a full-time writer: representing the family of a railroad brakeman killed when he was pinned between two cars.[6]

My body felt numb, my eyes not moving.

Pinned between two cars…

"Am I reading that correctly?" I thought as I sat up straighter and leaned in to where I could see better. Reading it again, not able to see anything else on the page, I thought, "Oh God, if that isn't You. No way is that a coincidence. No way."

In that moment, I felt I'd been given faith the size of a mustard seed (Matthew 17:20) and was placing it in an Almighty God. If there was faith that could tell a mountain to move into the sea or faith that could open up a sea and allow people to pass through on dry land, I felt I was grasping ahold of it. Then I knelt on the floor and prayed the biggest prayer I'd ever prayed, "God, this is not an accident. You have led me here. Lord, tell John Grisham I'm coming."

The story wove in and out of my mind as I sat up on the couch then again at night when I lay awake in bed.

Weeks passed, and I continued to write, adding on to each part of the story as it was unfolding. After Christmas, Michael left for his work for Costa. Michelle offered to come visit in mid-January during one of Michael's cruises—it was the perfect time for her too, as her husband was going on a pastor's retreat.

---

[6] "Bio." *JGrisham*. Penguin-Random House. www.JGrisham.com.

She arrived with her two kids, and we were ready for visitors! Thankfully, the sun was out, so the kids played in the yard while she and I drank coffee and visited. Talking about her recent move to a new town and their new church and about our adventures in Mountain View made for a nonstop conversational weekend.

My precious friend Michelle and me in our home in Mountain View

Visiting the candy shop on the square, we purchased taffy for the kids and fudge for ourselves. Loading the baby into the car, I turned to Michelle and said, "You'll never believe what I read on John Grisham's website."

"Really? What?" she asked as she got into the driver's side and put on her seatbelt.

"He's taken only one break in his writing career, and it was to represent a family in a trial. Guess what for?"

"I have no idea. What?"

"He was representing the family of a man who had died between two cars."

Silence. She moved her head slowly and looked over at me, "Are you kidding me?"

"No! I'm not! Can you believe that?"

"Rachel, yes, I can. I can believe that. Your story is so unbelievable that I'd believe anything you tell me right now."

She paused, looking out the window and taking a deep breath, "It's either God or the cruelest joke I've ever heard."

We sat in silence looking at the view as we drove up the hill, then she said, "John Grisham defended that man in his death. Ask him to defend you in your life."

Before she left, we had a time of prayer for all the events taking place in our lives.

"Go get your manuscript," she said.

Thankfully, I had printed out what I'd written so far, so I got it off my dresser then placed it on the living room floor.

"Let's lay our hands on it and pray," she suggested as we both knelt down and touched the edge of it. Then she began, "Lord, I thank you for the work that You are doing and are about to do through Rachel. We pray You will take this and use it, and if it be Your will, we pray it straight into John Grisham's hands. That he will take it and use it to further Your kingdom. We pray this in Jesus's name. Amen."

"Yes, Lord, let it be as Michelle said it would be. In Jesus's name. Amen."

"All right," she said as she gave me a hug, "Now let's watch and see what He does."

CHAPTER 17

I'd dropped off what I'd written at Mr. Grisham's house. I'd written his daughter's name on the envelope, but I was starting to think it wasn't for her—it was for John. I couldn't explain it, but it seemed certain events were taking place around him—so much so I thought about Michelle's prayer and began to wonder if I should give my manuscript directly to him.

The book was alive to me. I'd finish a chapter, God would perform another miracle, and then I would add it to the manuscript. It continued to play out, so the manuscript was always changing. I was always updating it—so that every week or two the latest chapters had to be printed and bound.

I asked friends and family to be praying and fasting for the book. Some I asked for prayers for the publication of the book, some I asked for prayers specifically for John. I could hardly text it without laughing:

Morning prayers at our house

"I need your prayers for this book, specifically for the publication of it, and will you also pray and fast for…"

I smiled as I typed it out:

"john grisham…"

"Maybe if I put it in all lowercase they won't know who I'm talking about," I said as I laughed out loud.

I was sure the thought of it probably seemed so far out, "But it's not. I serve an Almighty, Living God."

I edited, added pictures from our life and fiery ordeals, printed it out, and prayed over it. The phone rang. "Rachel," Michelle said, "In my prayer time this morning, I believe the Lord told me to share this with you—I think you need to prepare your heart to meet John Grisham."

I paused.

"You think so?"

"Yes, I do. I mean, I hesitated to say it at first, but after I got your text, I decided to go ahead and pass that message along."

Earlier that evening, while I was printing out pages from my manuscript, I had received a text from a friend asking us to come to dinner—her husband was making gumbo.

"The Fletchers asked us to come over for—get this— gumbo! Can you believe that? You know the last time we had gumbo, right? It was when we were in Louisiana—when the Lord first gave me the vision of the raft! Is that hilarious? God has the best sense of humor."

"Your story starts and ends with gumbo," Michael joked.

I texted the story to Michelle because I knew she would get a kick out of it, and then she called to tell me what the Lord had revealed to her. When I hung up with Michelle, I told Michael what she had said. Caroline walked in, caught the last of the story, and then chimed in, "Mom, God told me the same thing as I was standing at the sink washing my hands. You need to be ready to meet him."

"What?"

"Yep. Right now when I was in the kitchen washing my hands, God told me the same thing."

I'd thought many months about being re-baptized. God was doing such an incredible, supernatural work in my life, and I wanted to re-commit my life to Him and to His purposes. Before I got in the shower, I felt the Lord leading me to get baptized, right then and there. I went into the living room where Michael was sitting, "Hey, listen, the Lord is leading me to get re-baptized, and I want you to do it. I'd like to do it now. I feel like that's what He's telling me to do."

"Right now? Like in the bathtub?

"Yes, if that's okay."

I put on Michael's cruise ship robe and sat down in the water with my kids surrounding me. "I baptize you in the name of the Father and the Son and the Holy Spirit. Buried with Christ," he said as he submerged me in the water, "Raised to walk in newness of life."

I was talking with my mom on the phone the next day, "I'm sure everyone and their dog has tried to give a book to him. But for some reason, I think it's for him. That sounds stupid, doesn't it?"

"I don't know. I'm sure if the Lord wants you to do it, He'll make a way. After all, nothing is too difficult for Him" (Luke 18:27).

Although I was conflicted at times and went from faith to doubt to faith again, I thanked her for reminding me of the fact that God can do anything.

We were still talking when Caroline, who was sitting across from me said, "Mom, I just had another vision."

I hung up the phone, "Caroline, what? Mommy was on the phone. What is it?"

"While you were on the phone…I had another vision. You were standing with John Grisham at a book fair, and you were selling your books. And mom, there were angels standing over you like this," she explained as she brought her hands to an arch and touched them over her head.

"Caroline, that's unbelievable. God's really speaking to you right now isn't He?"

I pulled her over to me.

"Tell me, tell me what you saw."

"There were two angels."

"What did they look like?"

"They were white! White as snow," she insisted as she stood back from me and looked me in the eye, "and their shoes had gold ribbons and they had blue sashes around their waists."

I'd never heard her talk the way she'd been talking the last several weeks. But it was real and specific. And it caught my attention.

Michael had left for his work for Costa, and later that evening, I was in the kitchen making grilled cheese sandwiches for the kids. Caroline walked into the kitchen as I was putting butter in the skillet.

"Mom, you'll think this is funny."

"No, I won't. What?"

"No, I don't want to say," she replied as she scrunched up her face and tilted her head to the side.

"Caroline, I know you're hearing from the Lord. I won't think it's funny—promise."

"Well, there's one more thing I saw while you were at the book fair," she paused, "Jesus was standing next to you."

I put the spatula down and turned around to face her.

"I believe it," I cried as tears welled up in my eyes, "If there is someone who's doing all of this, it is definitely Him."

She drew a picture and brought it to me.

As I was finishing dinner, I picked up my phone to check Facebook. I knew Caroline had never seen John Grisham, so I brought up a picture of him to ask if he was the man in the vision. Before I could even ask her to look at it, she peered over my shoulder.

Caroline's drawing of her vision

"Yep, that's him. That's the man I saw in my vision."

CHAPTER 18

Spring arrived, and the dogwoods were in full bloom as were the pink and yellow wildflowers—it was truly a gorgeous season in the Ozark Mountains! I opened the doors and windows as I dusted the furniture and cleaned areas that had been barely touched since our move the previous year. Stopping to pick up an old sorority magazine that had fallen behind the couch, I flipped through its pages when I noticed a picture of three Chi Omegas standing with the first lady of Kentucky in the governor's mansion.

"Look closely at that picture."

I stared at it.

"Okay, God. What is it?"

"When they went to the governor's mansion, they were prepared."

That made sense. These three ladies were nicely dressed, smiling at the camera. They were not caught off guard. This was a meeting they knew was coming about and they probably spent ample time getting ready for it.

If I were like a modern-day Esther, what would I do to prepare? Spiritually, I felt God had prepared and was continuing to prepare my heart and my mind for such a meeting. Physically, I'd try to look my best. It had been a while since I had a haircut, so I thought having my hair and nails done seemed like an adequate task for preparation. I called the girl who had done my hair once before, but when the stylist who answered the phone said my girl was completely booked, I wasn't sure what to do.

"Are you sure? She doesn't have any openings today?"

"No ma'am. She can see you next week though."

"No, that won't work."

Silence.

"Okay God, you told me to prepare today," I thought as I looked at myself in the mirror and sat there, waiting.

"Well, I can do it for you!" the lady said.

"You can? Okay, great! Well, I have long hair and need a trim. Can you trim it?"

"Sure."

"And I'll probably get my nails done, as well. Do you have time for all of that?"

"Actually, yes. Can you be here in ten minutes?"

After I arrived, she washed my hair then sat me down in her chair and started trimming. I'd never met her before, so I was making small talk when she told me how blessed she was in her business.

"She's a Christian," I thought as I watched the hair fall onto the floor.

She continued on and then asked about how we ended up in Mountain View. By the time I'd finished talking about

Michael and how God had brought us to Arkansas, she was starting my toes.

"So, you're out treating yourself today?"

"Well, actually, the Lord told me to prepare, so I'm doing that."

I told her my own story of how I began a book when I'd arrived, how the church asked us to come to serve, how I'd met the Grisham family through those circumstances, and how I wondered if my manuscript was for John himself.

"I met them a long time ago. My parents were Gideons with his parents. You won't believe this, but the last several days, the Lord has given me the word, 'book,' and I had no idea what it meant. I even talked to my daughter and asked her, 'Why would God give me the word "book?" I don't want to write a book.' But now I know why. The Holy Spirit was giving me a prophetic word for you. He knew I was going to meet you."

By the time she started my fingernails, she had greatly encouraged me, and as she painted the clear polish on top of the pink, she stammered, "That's crazy. Right now, as I was painting your fingernails, the Lord gave me a vision of you handing him your manuscript. Literally...like with this hand."

"Really? You are the third person who has said something about giving it to him..." I didn't really know what else to say. God was bringing people from all around to speak into my life.

As I was walking that later evening, I was overcome with a reverence and a holy fear.

"You're doing something huge, something magnificent."

It made me want to fall on my face right there in the middle of the sidewalk. I lifted my hands to heaven, "God, You're pulling out all the stops. You've done so much."

It was a sacred holiness. I wanted to take my shoes off and relish the holy ground upon which I stood. I didn't really think what God was doing was about me or Michael or John Grisham. It was about Him. I wanted to share my story with the world He loves and share hope for those who have lost theirs. The words spilling out in my journal and onto the computer screen were about showing others God still moves like He did back in the Old Testament times because it was a miraculous thing He was doing. A miracle on display for all to see. I thought of stories from the Old Testament: fires, famines, earthquakes, walls falling with a shout (Joshua 6), entire armies being annihilated with a song (2 Chronicles 20), and I wanted to get on my face in reverence to a Holy God.

"You are the God of Old."

I pictured God swinging his strong and mighty arm, and the best spot for me to be was right by His side, out of the way, close enough to be protected, near enough to hear His voice, side-by-side to see Him work.

"Get out of the way."

"Yes, Lord, I will. Your word is going forth."

Later, we went down to the town square so Michael could pass out brochures for his upcoming show, but then it started to rain, and we decided to leave.

"Before we do, let's drive past the Grisham's...just to see," I suggested as he put on his seatbelt. "I've asked the Lord to show me when he's in town, and if he is, I'll take the book

114

over. This all still seems a little crazy, so that's what I asked! For God to clearly show me John's here. When that happens, I'll go! I prayed that this morning."

We turned the corner and drove a few blocks, pulling up closer to their home. At that exact moment, we saw a man walking into the house.

"That's him," Michael said calmly.

"You're kidding, right?"

"No, I think that's him."

I couldn't believe it. But then again, I could. I'd never seen him before, but I knew how God was continually putting His work on display as the all-powerful Miracle Maker. The miracles continued to shoot up toward heaven like a fireworks show.

"You told God if He'd let you know John was in town, you'd take your book over to him. Time to uphold your end of the bargain."

"Okay, I will, but I'm not ready, I have to add the most recent visions to the book."

"Well, get to workin' on it!"

Michael took the kids to eat dinner, and I brought my manuscript up-to-date.

"I want to take it over there and hand it directly to him like Caroline saw in her vision."

"Then take it on Sunday morning," Michael suggested as he put Mary Manor's pajamas on.

"Do you think I should go to the door even if there are no cars in the driveway?"

"That's up to you. I mean, if that's the sign you're looking for...but this is all in faith, Rachel, every single bit of it. I say go for it. You have nothin' to lose."

I thought to myself, "Alright, Lord. No matter what, I'm going to the door in total faith that whenever I knock, he's going to open it. After all, it's in Your word that the righteous will live by faith (Romans 1:17). Do You want to give me one more sign?"

"No more signs; walk by faith."

And that is what I did.

CHAPTER 19

Imagine my disappointment when no one answered the door.

I got back into the car, "Well, no answer."

"No one home?"

"Nope," I said as I put my book down next to my feet.

I was silent as we drove to church. My hope deflated. When we arrived, Michael and the kids went in while I sat down on a bench and looked out across the street. I felt stupid. Why was I even trying to do this? It seemed to be where God was leading, but why wasn't John there? Why would God send me friends and even strangers with words about placing a book into his hands if God wasn't going to bring it to pass? After mulling over it for a half of an hour, I thought of Hebrews 11:6, "And without faith it is impossible to please God, because anyone who comes to him must believe that he exists and that he rewards those who earnestly seek him" (NIV), so I prayed, "Lord, You said that without faith, it's impossible to please you, and God, in faith, I have stepped out. You also said that when we draw near to You, You'll draw near to us (James 4:8). Lord, draw near to me today, I pray. I'm disappointed with how this turned out. Really disappointed. If I am going the wrong direction, please don't send any more signs and wonders. Just let it end. But if this is what You want me to do, please continue to send confirmations—through your Word, through other people, through Your words to me…"

Even though it didn't go the way I'd expected, I had to believe it was pleasing to Him. Even if the result wasn't what I'd anticipated, at least I'd stepped out in obedience. But I still asked Him to carry it forward or remove it completely.

However, I was reminded there was a part of me I was still withholding from the Lord. A complete surrender of my fertility. I'd felt, since my days of working for the Catholic nuns, the Lord wanted me to leave our family planning totally in his hands. I'd never fully given it over to the Lord as I'd said I would. It was, for me, the last area in my life that was unsurrendered to the Lord. Pulling my Bible out of my purse, I was led to Isaiah 43:24, "…But you have burdened me with your sins and wearied Me with your offenses" (NIV).

For years, I had complained…expecting Him to answer my prayers…all the while, I was wearing Him out with my own sin. Like I explained to Michael, it was an area that was not surrendered. If God had told me to go to China, and I didn't, that would be an unsurrendered area. But this issue was the one I'd dealt with for ten years and had never completely let go of. As long as there was unsurrendered junk in my life, how could the Holy Spirit live His life through me? I talked with Michael after church about not holding back anymore. I was not in control. I told him I could not live holding anything back from God—He had to have it all and deserved nothing less than all. That day, I completely surrendered the one area about which I'd fought with the Lord for many years.

A month passed, and the day after Easter, I was on my face in prayer.

"Okay, Lord, I'm here. What do You want me to do?"

"Come nearer to Me. Go behind the veil."

I started reading about the veil in the Old Testament. It was used in the temple and separated the presence of God from the people, "...and the veil shall serve for you as a partition between the holy place and the holy of holies " (Exodus 26:33, NASB). The priest went beyond the veil to the Holy of Holies once a year to make a sacrifice for the people's sins, and when Christ died, the veil was torn in two (Matthew 27:51), allowing mankind a direct way to God through Jesus Christ (Hebrews 10:19-23). What the Lord showed me was His presence was essential. For me to live and walk in the way He was leading, I needed to let Him flow in me and through me, I needed to *live* in His presence. When I go behind the veil, I am hidden, and all that can be seen is Him.

The next two nights, I woke up at 2:30, and the Lord showed me specific people to ask for prayer besides the ones who already were praying.

"Get the army to march it forward."

The first night God led me to contact my college roommate Dana, my former boss from the Catholic college, and my Thursday morning Bible study group from Pulaski. I explained the story to each of them and asked for specific prayers for the book and for God's word to go forth. The second night I woke up after dreaming of being anointed with oil at a church I'd delivered posters to once for Michael. My mentor, JoAnne, came to mind as well as *The 700 Club* prayer line.

When I woke up that morning, I called the secretary at the church where I believed I should go to receive prayer. "When do your intercessory prayer warriors meet? I need to come and be anointed with oil and prayed over."

119

"They meet in an hour."

When I arrived, two women were already in the sanctuary and were expecting me as the secretary had told them I was coming. "We were told someone was coming today for prayer."

"Yes ma'am. I need to be anointed and prayed over. Can you do that?"

She proceeded to ask me what exactly I needed prayer for. She told me I could tell as much or as little of my story, having no idea what I was there for. I assured her it was a wonderful work that God was doing, and I was asking for completion, and I had woken up in the night feeling the need to be prayed over.

"Well, let's do it," she said as she went up to the altar to get the anointing oil.

"Can I come and get down on my face? That's what I think I need to do," I asked as I stood up from my seat.

"You can sit, stand, bow, whatever the Lord leads You to do."

I felt the overwhelming presence of the Holy Spirit. I took my sandals off, walked down to the altar, and got on my knees as she opened the vial. She put the oil on my forehead as the other woman walked up toward me. When she moved her hands to my shoulders, I placed my face on the ground.

Then the prayers began—and it felt like we were ushered straight into the presence of God—like an immersion in the Holy Spirit's fire.

"Lord, You have a plan and a calling on this young lady's life, and we pray You would bring the vision to pass. Baptize her in Your Spirit. Confirm what You are doing. You are raising up people everywhere with a passion for You. She is one but not the only one. She is one of many people who are hungering and thirsting for You. For Your Kingdom to come and Your will to be done..."

Then I felt compelled to pray. "Can I pray for y'all, too?"

"Yes, absolutely."

After I left, I called my friend and mentor JoAnne and told her the entire story and asked for prayer.

"You have my word on it. In fact, I'm going to start a novena. It's nine days of powerful intercessory prayer, and I'm going to do that for you."

"You know I love you. You've always been such a powerful person in my life."

"I love you, too. I'm praying!"

My next and final call for the day was to *The 700 Club* prayer line. I was putting clothes away in my closet when a lady answered, "Good afternoon, 700 club prayer line."

We exchanged greetings then she asked, "First of all, can I ask you about your relationship with Christ?"

"Yes ma'am, I'm a born-again believer."

"Alright, awesome. What can I pray with you about today?"

"Well, I was actually one of the testimonials on your show last week."

"Is that right?"

"Yes, ma'am. I survived being crushed between two cars several years ago, and y'all filmed my story several years ago. Interestingly enough, you aired it again last week."

"Oh, my goodness. What a remarkable story."

I proceeded to tell her how God had used that exact story again in my life, about our move to Arkansas, and about the commonality the story shared with John Grisham. I told her about the book I felt the Lord leading me to write and asked her to pray for God's will to be done and, if God willed, that it would land in John Grisham's hands.

"Okay, let's pray."

She began to pray as I got on my knees in my closet.

Then she stopped in the middle of her prayer.

"Oh, hallelujah, hallelujah, hallelujah."

My countenance began to break. I put my head down as the tears flowed down my cheeks.

"Hallelujah, hallelujah, oh hallelujah, thank you, Jesus..." she went on to say several more times.

That evening, as I was going to pick up Micah from baseball practice, I felt the Lord leading me to do one more thing that day. The Catholics were praying, and the charismatics were, too. Now I needed to come before my own church and ask for prayer.

"Lord, what do you want me to say?"

"Tell them the Lord did bring you to their church."

"Okay, God. Show me what to say, and I'll say it."

"Tell them their pastor heard from the Lord and ask for prayer for what is about to go forth."

That night, I went by myself to church. After we ate, Pastor Roger took prayer requests, as usual, and I waited until the end when he asked if there were any more.

"Pastor, I have something I'd like to say."

"Yes, Rachel, what's that?"

"Well, I want you all to know that some may think it's been awkward for us ever since the job thing with Michael. But I want you all to know your pastor did hear from God, and God did want us here at this church." A couple of people turned around and smiled at me, so I continued on. "I want to ask for prayer for our family and the direction the Lord wants us to go. I'd also like to ask for prayer for a book I started when I moved here that I believe God wanted me to write. Will you please pray it into the right person's hands?"

"Yes, we will. And we are so glad you guys are here with us. God does have a very special plan for your family," Pastor Roger stated as he looked at me from the podium.

Then he continued on, "Let's turn to Ecclesiastes 3 where we will continue our study. 'To everything there is a season, and a time for every matter under heaven: a time to be born, and a time to die; a time to plant, and a time to pluck up what is planted; a time to kill, and a time to heal...'" (Ecclesiastes 3:1-3a, NIV).

I looked down at the text, "...a time to kill..."

"Isn't that the name of one of Grisham's novels?" I thought as I turned my head and laughed, softly.

"Lord, it's too much. Really, You are personal, Jesus."

CHAPTER 20

I'd let another friend of mine read my book. She'd read the first few chapters, and I assured her God changed me throughout the text and to keep reading. I had not added on past the point of a hopeful delivery of the book, so that is as far as she got. When she e-mailed me, she said, "I liked it, but are you sure this is what you should do?"

"Well, remember, you haven't read what God has done these past several months, it's been very supernatural," I wrote back.

"Yes, I get that, but do you know what you're getting into? I mean, John Grisham is pretty powerful, and I bet it'd be hard to get this to him."

There seemed to be a sense of fear in what she was saying.

"Well, this is where God has led me, and I'm trying to be obedient."

But the next day, I started to worry. Maybe I shouldn't try to get this to him. After all, people who knew him said I wouldn't be able to do it. I got down on my face during my prayer time and heard,

"Rachel, why are you turning to the right and to the left, following other gods and serving them?" (Deuteronomy 28:14).

"What gods, Lord?"

"Other people's opinions."

The Lord showed me it was His voice and His instruction I needed to follow.

Several days had passed when I started thinking about calling Everett, an agent I'd met while living in Tennessee.

"I believe God is going to bring about the delivery, but I don't know how He's going to do it," I said to Michael one night as we sat on our porch. "I think I'm going to call Everett and get his take on it."

"What do you think he'll say?"

"I don't know, but I guess I can ask. Maybe he'll give me some direction or advice on how to go about this…"

I spoke with Everett for an hour and a half, telling him everything that had led me up to the road I was about to take.

"It's a very, very interesting story," he agreed, "and I definitely want to read it, so please send it to me."

"Okay."

"There are two people that are coming to my mind, both with Thomas Nelson. So, I'd like to talk to them about this and get their feedback—maybe that'll give you some direction—and let them read it as well."

"Okay, that'd be great. Thank you."

"Sure. Send it to me, and I'm going to pray for you before we hang up."

He did, and I told Michael what he'd said after I'd gotten off the phone.

"Well, I still have more work to do on it, 'cause I'm not finished with it, but he said to go ahead and send it."

"Whatever you think the Lord wants you to do," he replied.

I decided to wait before I sent it, so I slept on it that night. The next day, Micah had an out of town game, and the girls had softball games. So I took Micah to his, and Michael took the girls to theirs. Micah was tired from getting up early, so he was sitting quietly in the backseat, and I was going back and forth over what I should do with the book.

"Lord, I'm confused. I think this is for John Grisham, and I don't want to go in a direction You are not leading me."

I continued driving, looking out at the rolling hills of the Ozarks, when I heard in my spirit,

"The next one to read it is John Grisham."

And with that word from the Lord, I felt peace and joy. And I stood in faith that God was going to get this manuscript to him, as I looked forward to another miracle unfolding.

CHAPTER 21

Michael's parents, Mimi and Pappy, were missing the kids, so Michael and I decided to meet them in Memphis and let them take the kids for the weekend.

Not wanting to waste time, I pulled out my laptop and continued writing on my story. Over the course of that weekend, I wrote for about twenty hours. Then when I'd taken the story as far as I could, I placed it in a manila envelope and set it by the back door.

I prayed, "Okay, Lord. Show me John Grisham's in town, and, once again, I'll take it to him."

A few weeks later, the kids were having an end-of-year ceremony at church. Sitting down in the pew, I placed my purse beside my feet and pulled out a stick of gum.

"How are you?"

I glanced up to see Karen standing in front of me.

"Good, girl, how's it going?" I asked.

"Good. We've been busy. Ooohh, I'm tired."

"Yeah? Whatcha been up to?"

"Well, we were in Little Rock yesterday, and today we visited a couple of folks and then ran errands this afternoon."

128

"Karen," I heard someone say from across the aisle. She turned and walked toward the woman, leaving me sitting in the pew.

"Okay, Lord, I'm totally trusting You," I thought.

"Kids all ready?" Michael asked as he sat down next to me.

"Yeah, they're in their classrooms with their teachers."

Pastor Roger walked over and shook Michael's hand as I looked over the awards pamphlet.

"Hey, man, how's it going?" Michael asked.

"Good, good. We've been busy," he said.

"Yeah, what've y'all been doing?"

"Well, we had to go to Little Rock yesterday. Then today we visited some folks around town," he paused then continued on, "Yeah, it's Mr. Grisham's birthday today, so all his kids are in town…"

My heart started to race.

I looked up at Pastor Roger.

"All his kids are in town…" the words echoing in my mind.

The pastor walked off, and I looked over at Michael, "I knew He would do it."

After the service, Michael and I were watching the kids on the playground behind the church. "Rachel, I don't think it would be appropriate to go over tonight, not on Mr. Grisham's birthday. Go in the morning. The timing needs to be right."

"I agree. I don't want the delivery to be awkward."

We had to run by the theater on our way home, and as I stood at the concession stand, waiting for Michael to set up his props, I texted a few friends and asked for prayer.

My hair stylist, immediately wrote me back, "Man, I love when I have a breakthrough, and although it's you, I feel blessed to watch it come through for you. God is soooo good! Okay, bear with me here because I never wanna overstep my bounds with the Holy Spirit, but I wrote that to you and immediately bowed my head to pray. I felt and heard it at the same time. It almost felt audible, but I know it wasn't. But I heard the words, 'I'm already doing it,' and as fast as I opened my eyes, I heard myself say, 'He's taken care of it.' It was like I got hit with an epiphany. One of those moments where it comes out of nowhere and it shakes me to the core. Like when I told you about the book. I got that same feeling."

After the kids were in bed, I walked downstairs to the living room.

"Okay, I have a verse for you," Michael said as he looked up at me. "The Lord gives the command; The women who proclaim the *good* tidings are a great host: 'Kings of armies flee, they flee, And she who remains at home will divide the spoil!'" (Psalm 68:11-12 NASB).

"No way!" I exclaimed. "I read that this morning!"

"Then that's your confirmation. You're that woman, the woman who's proclaiming good news. That lady who is going forward, doing what God has told you. Telling others about Him."

I heard Mary Manor crying upstairs, so I went upstairs to check on her and found her lying on her back, wailing.

"Hey sweet girl, what's wrong?" I held her as we rocked then laid her back down in her bed. She started crying again, so I placed my hands on her chest and began to pray.

"Lord Jesus, I ask you to calm her down, help her to sleep well, I pray."

"A mighty rushing wind..."

The phrase had come to me for several days and had come again while I was praying for Mary Manor, and I was reminded about how the Holy Spirit came like a mighty rushing wind on the day of Pentecost (Acts 2:2).

"Mighty Rushing Wind, I ask You to come and blow over this house, blow over me and my family, blow over this city, this nation, this world...Holy Spirit come in power, come with Your fire and burn us up, I pray."

I continued to pray as I placed my hands on her chest. Then I began to pray in the Spirit, a language I had received when I was a child and filled with the Holy Spirit after receiving Jesus Christ as my savior. As I prayed, I thought of Mark 16:17, "These signs will follow those who have believed...they will speak with new tongues..." (NASB).

Her crying stopped as the words flowed out of me. I wasn't aware of what I was saying, but I knew the Spirit knew and understood, "For one who speaks in a tongue does not speak to men but to God; for no one understands, but in *his* spirit he speaks mysteries" (1 Corinthians 14:2, NASB).

131

Then I continued, "Mighty Rushing Wind, come in Your power. Violent Rushing Wind, come blow over Your people, come that Your work will be done on Earth as it is in Heaven," I continued to pray with intensity and with a holy fear, not aware of time passing—being enveloped in His presence.

My eyes were closed.

Then, something like I'd never seen before.

A bright flash of light. The brightest I'd ever seen. It was like someone had taken a camera with a strobe light and flashed it right in my face.

"Whoa," I stammered as I completely opened my eyes and looked up, almost afraid at what I would find. "What was that?"

The room was still dark.

"Oh, Lord, You *are* here."

CHAPTER 22

"Alright, today's the day; it's delivery day," I said as I opened my eyes and took my glasses from the bedside table. The first verse on my mind was Isaiah 55:12, "For you will go out with joy And be led forth with peace; The mountains and the hills will break forth into shouts of joy before you, And all the trees of the field will clap *their* hands" (NASB).

Before I left, Michael and the kids laid their hands on me and prayed for me. I gave them each a hug and a kiss and assured them that this was a work we all shared in.

But when I reached their house, there was no one there. Again.

My spirit was crushed.

"Okay, God, what's up with that?" I asked as I got back into the car and turned the corner, my manuscript shifting in the seat.

I drove around the block and continued nervously.

"I'll drive around and pray; maybe they'll show back up."

I stopped for a minute to text my mom and sister, both of whom I knew were praying, and told them no one was home. I also texted a couple of friends and told them the same thing. One or two texted back with encouraging words and told me to not give up.

"But I feel so stupid," I thought as I drove past some of the first places we'd visited when we came to Mountain View.

After a little while, I drove back by the house again—there were still no cars.

"Lord, I don't get You. I keep putting my heart out there and putting my heart out there. I feel like You're stomping on it. You tell me to finish it, show me he's here, and then I miss him. What do You want me to do?"

After I came home, I told the kids what had happened. They didn't seem worried about it, but I was. I didn't understand what God was doing. I felt I'd been in labor with this thing for many months, and either I needed to give birth to it, or I might die on the delivery table. I was confused and frustrated.

I thought, "I didn't ask to be here. I didn't ask for this to be my story. This is where God has led me. Don't you see it? This is what He has done, not me. But if He wants this to go forth, He has to bring it, not me. I continue to obey and continue to obey and on and on, and then I feel defeated. I don't know what to do."

And the day continued to spiral downward from there. I needed time alone. I needed clarity and peace. But it was not coming.

So, I waited.

My brain needed a break, so I started to read a book called, *Living on the Devil's Doorstep* by Floyd McClung. I had downloaded it on my Kindle and decided to delve into it.

It was a story of a missionary family who followed Jesus into Amsterdam, followed Him right into the Red-Light District. The opening scene was of a funeral procession. As crowds gathered and the district's main thoroughfares became crowded, the man, Floyd, began to preach. And as he preached, the Lord began showing him things about one man in the crowd in particular. Floyd went on to say that God showed him the man in the crowd was married with three children at home. So, he asked the man why he was there in the Red Light District when he was married with kids.

"The Lord gave Floyd a specific, prophetic word for this man."

The man gave no answer, so Floyd began to address the crowd. He went on to say that despite all their lustful and hateful thoughts and deeds, God loved them so much that He came to earth and died on a cross. He told them how much God cared.[7] As I continued to read for what seemed like hours, the Holy Spirit was moving in me. What this family witnessed and lived was so real, so God.

What God was doing for me was real, too. I had seen miracles for the first time in my life. God was alive and active. More than that—He was powerful and mighty. Witnessing His power in ways I'd never been aware of made me wonder—had He always moved like this and I didn't notice it? Had He poured a new anointing on me? Whatever it was, I didn't want it to stop. If it was a river, I never wanted out but desired to be right in the center of it. Right in the middle of the rushing water. Back down on earth, the results I anticipated weren't happening as I expected, but the thrill of seeing the Holy Spirit like I'd never known was a spiritual high like none other. My focus was

---

[7] McClung, Floyd. *Living on the Devil's Doorstep: From Kabul to Amsterdam*. YWAM Publishing, 1999.

changing. And had been changing for two years. The Spirit was awakening in me and was growing more intense with each passing day. It seemed to be multiplying, even exponentially. It seemed fresh and new, and I wanted more of it.

As the days passed, my focus became less and less on getting a book delivered and more on the Holy Spirit being alive in me, truly pulling me up out of a watery grave like God had told me He would do and truly resurrecting me like God had told me He would do.

CHAPTER 23

Michael was performing a show at a church an hour south of Mountain View. He'd asked me to share my *700 Club* clip then talk a few minutes, and I'd agreed. When we arrived at the church, he went in to set up his props, and I sat in the car and asked the Lord what He wanted me to say. I started writing down notes about His power and found some verses to share, too. Because my car story was so miraculous, it led the way into talking about miracles and asking the congregation to pray for them in their own lives.

When the show began, I felt confident in what I was to say. When I was in front of the congregation I said, "You know a reason I think God loves doing miracles? Because He gets all the glory for it when it happens! When it's something outside of man's reach, something no person can do, and He gets it done—He puts Himself on display. And He receives all the glory."

After the show, I was packing up some of my children's books in the lobby when I saw Michael walking over to me.

"Hey, Rachel," he said as motioned for a young lady to come over to us, "this is Christina, and she has been diagnosed with cancer. I was telling her about our belief in gifts of healing, and I think you should lay your hands on her and pray for her."

My heart started beating faster.

Never in all of our years of traveling together had he ever put me on the spot like that and asked me to pray for a miracle for someone.

"Uh, yeah, we can do that," I said as I put the books into the box.

"Ok, great, and I'll get the kids to come pray, too," he stated as he turned toward the sanctuary.

When all our kids arrived in the lobby, the young lady's grandmother had come over, too. There were a lot of people walking around, so I asked, "Why don't we step over here into the nursery and pray?"

We did, and I asked the young lady about her situation.

"Well, I'm thirty, have two young kids, and I was diagnosed with appendix cancer a few months ago. I went in for what I thought was an ovarian cyst, and they found malignant tumors in several spots. I've already had surgery, but I have to have more, and I'll be going to M.D. Anderson in Houston in a few weeks."

As she was speaking, I felt the Holy Spirit overcoming me. I wondered if He was about to do a miracle in her life, for her and her family, for us and our family, and for the glory of His name.

"Well if it's okay with you, I'd like to lay my hands on you and pray for you. Can you show me where your appendix is?" I asked as I smiled, feeling silly that I had no idea where an appendix was.

"Sure, right here," she said as she placed her hand on her lower abdomen.

"Alright kids, circle up. We're going to pray for Ms. Christina that the Lord would completely heal her of cancer."

I placed one hand on her stomach and one on her shoulder. The kids also put their hands on her back, arms, wherever they could reach. Michael placed his hand on her shoulder and her grandmother held her hands.

I couldn't even start to pray.

Tears welled up in my eyes, ran down my face. I stood there, speechless, overwhelmed by the Lord. I could not say one word.

Caroline looked over at me and whispered, "Mom, are you going to pray?"

Then the words came.

"Lord, Jesus, thank You for Christina and the work You're doing in her life. Thank You for the children You've given her. I pray You would bless her with a long life to raise these precious kids. I pray over this cancer in Jesus's name—that You would take it away right now and heal her. I've seen so many miracles in my own life, and now I'm praying for one for my sister in the Lord. Your Word says these signs will follow those who believe—that in Your name we will lay our hands on the sick and they will recover (Mark 16:17-18). Lord, we believe that when she goes to the doctor, they will find no cancer. Heal her and restore her. We pray this in Jesus's name, Amen."

I placed my face in my hands and wiped away all the tears. I looked up and gave her a hug.

"Thank you so much," she said.

"Absolutely, girl! The verse I was talking about is from Mark 16. So, I believe God can do this! Let's keep in touch."

"Yeah, that sounds good. You on Facebook?"

"Yes. You? What's your full name?"

She gave it to me, and later that night, I added her so I could keep up and see what the doctors said at her next appointment.

June arrived, and we'd signed the kids up for the Mountain View kids' swim team, which meant practice every day and swim meets on the weekends, which we occasionally attended. The practices were usually only an hour, so one afternoon I decided to take the kids early so they could have more time in the pool. All four kids were with me; the older three were swimming freely, and Mary Manor was attached to my hip. I was taking her around the pool, letting her splash and kick, and then taking her back to the stairs to let her sit.

On the steps, I was looking around at the crowd, and I thought to myself, "Jesus, if you were here in Mountain View today, You'd probably be hanging out at the pool." I loved stories from the Bible where Christ was out and about…with the people. He withdrew to pray and be alone, but He was also in the public places…with the people.

Mary Manor wanted to go back and forth from the big pool to the kiddie pool, so that's what we did. As I walked toward the kiddie pool, I noticed a young man sitting under the awning staring blankly at the ground. His hair was long and scraggly; his face seemed to be wreathed in sorrow—almost as if I could see the word "rejected" written across his countenance. My heart was pricked.

I continued to play with the kids, going from one pool to the next, taking breaks, and eating snacks, yet I was still aware of the young man who sat several feet behind me.

"The next time I walk past, I'll smile at him."

I tried, but he was still staring blankly at the pavement. He'd get up, go up to the concessions or locker room, and then come and sit back in the same place, shoulders hung low. Finally, I started to pray for him.

"Lord, I pray for that young man and whatever issues he may be facing. Help him."

Time continued to pass, and we were getting hot and tired. I decided to let Mary Manor have one more dip in the kiddie pool. I was sitting on the edge, holding her between my legs when I saw the young man walking, once again, toward his chair.

"Okay, Lord, do you have something you want me to say to him?"

"Tell him I have a plan for his life."

My breathing got heavier, my pulse faster.

I'd ask God for things like this then be surprised when He'd answer me.

"Tell him You have a plan for his life?"

"Tell him I have a plan for his life."

In spite of being in the water, my palms were getting sweaty.

"Help me. You know this makes me nervous—all this new stuff You're doing."

I got up and walked over and stood next to the fence where he was sitting, trying to make eye contact with him, but nothing happened. There was a lady sitting a few feet away.

"Lord, please let her move so I don't have to talk in front of her, too."

But she didn't.

After several minutes, other kids came up and stood in between us, sitting beside him and blocking my view of him. I felt my opportunity had passed. Mary Manor got out of the pool, and I decided it was time to go. I packed up my bags while keeping my eye on the young man, seeing if I could somehow get the courage up to go back over to him. He then stood up, got his stuff together, and walked past the gate, past the pool, and out the exit.

I was deflated.

I gathered our stuff together, told the other kids I'd pick them up after their swim lessons, scooped up Mary Manor, and headed out as well.

Putting my bags into the car, I was disappointed in myself.

"Lord, I was so lame just then! You gave me a word for someone, and I was too scared to deliver it. Forgive me; You know I'm human," and then I asked, "give me another chance, and I'll do it."

After strapping in, I drove past the baseball fields and was almost to the exit of the park when I saw the young man standing by a set of bleachers.

I drove past him because I was still so nervous then pulled over and put a towel around me.

"I'm not letting it pass me up again," I declared as I turned the car around.

I pulled up next to the sidewalk and rolled down my window.

"Excuse me, sir."

He turned around and looked at me.

"Yes, you. Hey! Can you come here real quick?" I asked as I motioned him over to the car. He came, his camouflage shorts hanging low, his arms swaying back and forth.

"Hey! How are you?" I asked as I stuck out my hand out the window, "I'm Rachel Kelley."

"I'm Travis," he replied as he shook my hand. His eyes looked deep, and his purple hair gleamed in the sun.

"Listen, I just saw you over at the pool, remember?"

He didn't say anything, so I continued on.

"Well, anyway, I saw you over there, and I was praying for you. And this is what I felt the Lord told me to tell you: He has a plan for your life," and as soon as the words left my mouth it was like taking a brick out of a dam, once the Spirit started to move, there was no stopping Him. "He has a plan for you. He's not forgotten about you. Be encouraged today. He's with you.

He's never leaving you. He has a great plan for your life. Don't ever forget that."

His eyes were holding on to mine strongly, steadily.

"Okay?"

"Yes ma'am, okay. Thank you."

"Well, He's done it. Not me. When I was sitting at the pool, I asked if He had a word for you, and that's what He told me to tell you. Then you left before I told you, and He gave me another chance to see you. That's awesome, isn't it."

"Yeah, thank you."

"Can I pray for you before I leave?"

"Sure."

I took his hands into mine and prayed, and before I drove off I continued, "Alright, Travis, I love you, and I'm going to be praying for you."

"I love you, too," he said as he let go of my hands and stepped back from the car.

It was a high like none other. The Bible says to not be drunk on wine but be filled with the Spirit (Ephesians 5:18), and it was no joke! It was a rush like I'd never experienced.

CHAPTER 24

Michael and I decided to take the kids on a weekend trip to Branson hoping to find theater connections for him, and while we were there, we visited a church. After the service was over, there was a time for people to come to the front and receive prayer. The pastor was still standing at the front of the sanctuary when he said, "I have a prophetic word for a lady here, and I hope it's okay to give that now."

Feeling my blood pressure soar, I wondered if it was going to be me.

"When I was up on stage singing, the Holy Spirit gave me a prophecy for this lady here," he stated as he looked me in the eyes and pointed. "Is it okay for me to give this to you?"

"Absolutely," I agreed as I could hear my heart pounding.

He walked over to me and prophesied, "Young lady, you're coming out of a deep valley, and Jesus wants you to know He is the Rose of Sharon" (Song of Solomon 2:1), he said as I nodded my head. "But He has anointed you, and He's going to use you. Do you believe that?"

"Yes, sir, I do," as tears started coming down my cheeks.

"But I feel called to pray against a spirit of chaos. I've never prayed that over anyone, but I'm going to pray against chaos."

"Yes, sir, thank you," I cried as I wiped my hands on my skirt.

"There is a trainload of blessings coming for you. It's carload after carload of blessings. When you hear the sound of the train coming, know that it's coming for you, and it's full of blessings."

The tears were falling so quickly I could not wipe them away fast enough.

"Can I pray for you?" he asked.

"Yes, please."

I was so touched by what God had done for me in that place. We'd come to Branson for theater connections, but God had reached down into that church service and had showered love on me personally and specifically.

When we got home Wednesday night, I brought up Facebook, and the first post I saw was from Christina, the young woman for whom I'd prayed healing from cancer:

"I want to thank everyone for all your prayers!!!! God is Good, God is great!!!! The prayers have been answered!!!! The spots that the Dr. saw before are gone! I am cancer free!!! All the glory goes to Him!!!!"

I ran to the back bedroom to tell Michael.

"You're not going to believe this! You know the Christina girl we prayed for?"

"Yeah?"

"She posted that she went to the doctor and that the cancer's gone!"

He started clapping his hands, and the kids came running!

"Kids, remember the lady we prayed for at the church? The one with cancer? Guess what. She went to the doctor, and it's gone!"

They were smiling and staring at me as they walked down the stairs.

"It's gone?"

"Yes, you guys, we've all witnessed a miracle!"

CHAPTER 25

Before I went to bed, I told Michael I wanted to write a letter to John Grisham and send it to an address I'd found online. "It sounds like a long shot, and I'm sure he's inundated with mail, but I'll send what I've written so far."

The next morning at 7:30 a.m., my phone rang as I walked into the kitchen.

"Melinda?" I thought as I saw the name on the screen. She was a friend of mine from Tenneesee, and I hadn't talked to her in months. I thought it was odd that she was calling so early.

"Hey, girl!" I said as I put coffee in the filter.

"Hey, Rach."

"Whatcha doing so early?"

"I have a word for you."

"Okay, bring it," I stated as I walked out of the kitchen and toward our bedroom.

"I'm driving down I-65, and I know it's early, but the Lord told me to call you and give you this word. I've been wrestling with Him for five minutes, but I'm giving in."

"No, it's awesome, sister. Bring it!"

"Rest. God wants you to rest in Him. Don't be stressed out about your book; don't worry about it. Just rest. He is going to bring it forth."

I loved the timing of her call, and since I had not talked to her in several months, I brought her up to date on the book and told her about the letter I planned to send.

"So, I'm not sure that God wants me to rest by taking naps all day," I chuckled.

"No ma'am. Get in your car and go to the post office, but ultimately, He's going to bring it to pass. And you're supposed to rest and not stress."

With that in mind, I opened up my laptop. I put my head in my hands and said a quick, silent prayer. Then I began my letter. I wrote the driveway story, and then I went on to tell of our financial struggles, being at the bottom, praying for a raft, and burying our talents in the backyard. I wrote about the resurrection of the *Costa Concordia*, our move to Mountain View, and the first time we set foot in his dad's church. I told him about our pastor recommending I talk with his family about my book, the word that both Michelle and Caroline had given to me concerning meeting him, and the day I looked at his bio page. Adding the most recent miracles, I printed out the letter, placed it on top of the chapters I'd written, put it in a box, and then took it to the post office.

I thought as I drove, "I haven't read anything of his in fifteen to twenty years. I wouldn't have known who he was six months ago if he were standing in a room with me. But I don't think this is all coincidental. I think the Lord's led me here."

Several weeks passed without a word, and one night as I sat around the dinner table with Michael and the kids, my feelings began to change.

"So, you're going to take it to that agent instead?" Micah asked.

"Well, yeah. People keep telling me John won't read it," I explained as I scooped sauce onto his plate of noodles.

He picked up his fork, looked at me, and asked, "Does God lie?" in all child-like honesty.

I paused, "Well, no He doesn't" (Numbers 23:19).

"Didn't God say that John Grisham was the next to read it?" he asked as he twirled the spaghetti around his utensil.

"Um, yeah, I think that's what He said, but I don't know. I'm confused."

"So, what're you gonna do, Mom? Obey people or obey God?" Camille asked looking straight into my soul with her delicate blue eyes.

I looked over at Michael, but the longer I sat at the dinner table, listening to all of it, the more troubled I became.

Chaos.

"I guess I can send the agent a few chapters. If John's supposed to read it next, then that's different than sending the entire book," I suggested to Michael while cleaning up the dishes.

"It sounds like you shouldn't make any decisions. You need clarity and peace. Wait until you know that whatever you do is what God has led you to do," he said. He knew I was troubled.

A few days later I was talking with Michelle on the phone. "I feel this whole thing is built on faith, and if I step out and try to make it happen, like the old Rachel would do, I might be stepping outside His will."

"Rachel, I have a total peace about what you're saying right now. Standing in faith that God's going to do what He's said is a wise decision."

"I know what I've heard from people who know him, and every time I think 'This is crazy. John Grisham is a huge author,' you know what the Lord says to me?"

"What?"

"No one can withstand the power of the Mighty Rushing Wind."

She prayed for me, and after we hung up, I decided to continue to wait.

"Everett asked for the manuscript weeks ago, and I need to know what to do. Please, God, show me."

I took the kids to a birthday party the next day, and when we got home, I felt that I was the one who needed to close the door with Everett. To do so would be to take a step away from the natural realm, one in which I could try to make something happen in my small human strength, and step toward the supernatural realm, one in which only God could make the impossible possible. So, before I got out of the car, I sent him a message:

151

"Everett, thank you so much for your offer, but I feel the Lord leading me to hold on to the manuscript for now. He's moving me in a different direction. I'll keep you posted on the story, and I thank you for all your prayers."

My walk was becoming a walk of faith, not of sight (2 Corinthians 5:7).

Michael was home on a short break from his shows, so I ran in and asked if I could run to Wal-Mart and pick up a pizza for dinner.

"Sure."

I grabbed my keys and headed back out the door.

I felt free. I felt light.

I pulled into a space and headed in. After grabbing dinner, I walked toward the check-out line when my senses heightened.

"Lord, if there is someone here who needs a word from You, show me," I prayed as I approached the cashier.

"How're you?" I asked her as I smiled.

"Good, you?"

"Good."

Nothing came.

I walked out the door and was almost in the parking lot when I heard a voice behind me. "How are you ma'am?"

I turned around to see a lady standing by a booth that said something about crisis counseling. I recognized it because I'd talked to them before.

"Hey, is this Dave Wilkerson's ministry? The pastor who wrote *The Cross and the Switchblade?*"

"Yes, it is," the lady said as she smiled at me, her blonde hair brushing her shoulders.

"Have you read that book?" I asked.

"No ma'am. I'm sure it's good. They have us reading a different book right now, along with the Bible, but we plan to read it soon.

"Awesome," I said as I stood in front of her and dug through my purse for some money.

"We're actually working on memorizing part of John 14 right now. Um, let's see if I can 'member some of it," she paused, "Believe Me that I'm in the Father and the Father's in Me; He who believes in me…let's see if I can remember, it's something about doing great works or something," her voice trailing off.

I chimed in, "Something about greater works we'll do because He sends us the Holy Spirit." (John 14:11-13).

"Yes! That's it," she said excitedly.

"Yeah, that's awesome." My heart started beating faster.

"I'm going to restore the years the locusts have eaten" (Joel 2:25).

My ears open, the Lord strongly impressed on me to tell her these words.

"Yeah, I've been in the program for a few months, and it's been good for me."

"What's your name?"

"Sienna." The lines her face told their own story.

"Sienna," I said as I set the pizza down on the table, "I have a prophetic word for you." Though many hard years disguised her brokenness, Sienna's eyes welled up with tears. "Is that okay?" I asked.

She shook her head up and down, biting her lip.

"Sienna, the Lord is going to restore the years the locusts have eaten" (Joel 2:25).

A tear fell down her face. She reached up to wipe her cheek, her hand shaking.

"Yes, He is," she agreed as she looked down, still wiping.

"He's going to restore the years the locusts have eaten. These years that you think you wasted? God's going to use them because He's awesome like that. He uses it all for His glory; He'll make it better than it ever was before."

"Yes, yes He will."

"Can I pray for you?"

"Please."

I did, and when we were finished, she hugged me.

"Thank you so much, you don't know how much that means to me. I'm forty-six years old, and I've never opened a Bible until recently. He's changing my life."

"Amen, sister, that's what He does."

We hugged again; I gave my donation to the lady and picked up my pizza.

"God bless you."

"God bless you, too."

When I got home, I was telling the kids what the Lord had done at Wal-Mart.

"Isn't it awesome? What God's doing?"

"Mom, you've changed a lot. Ever since you started writing that book, you've changed," Caroline observed as she looked at me from across the table.

Later that night I thought about her words and the truth in them, and I continued to look forward to all God was doing and was going to do. I thanked Him for the changes He was making in me and in our family. It was more than a book. More than meeting another author. It was about God and God alone. His power. His strength. His love. So, I sat there. Thinking. Knowing. Believing. That truly...

No one can withstand the power of the Mighty Rushing Wind.

CHAPTER 26

After our annual trip to San Antonio for July 4th, we returned home and resumed our daily schedule of playing, swimming, and Vacation Bible School. We'd recently found out we were expecting our fifth child, so while I was trying to get plenty of rest, the Lord was graciously giving me energy to keep up with my daily tasks. There were no doctors in Mountain View who delivered babies, so I was seeing a doctor about an hour away in Mountain Home. I was progressing just fine and thankful for good health for both the baby and me.

One morning I received a message from my hairdresser:

"Happy Monday morning soul sista'! So, the Father has put you on my mind. You flitted across my mind this past week more than usual. I got up around 4:30 this morning, which isn't really normal, and I spent time praying and reading the Word. You almost literally floated before my eyes. So, I got on my knees and talked to the Father about your situation and asked for 'something' today. After spending time in prayer, I got up to find out what was on Daystar or TBN. Every morning I watch it, but being up this early, you can't ever tell. I was clicking through the channels when I saw the name, 'John Grisham.' I watched what was left, and he was talking about his book and writing in general. Nothing major. But what are the chances? Girl, don't give up...read Rev. 3:7-8. Love you, woman! Press in!!"

I stirred the oatmeal and set my phone down. Grabbing my Bible, I turned to Revelation 3:7-8. "...Behold, I have put before you an open door which no one can shut, because you have a little power, and have kept My Word, and have not denied My name" (Revelation 3:8, NASB).

After swim lessons that afternoon, I told Michael I was going to run into town and get something to eat when Michelle texted me:

"Can I call you in a few?"

When I got in the car, I called her instead.

"Hey! What's up?"

"I'm on my way to Kroger and realized I forgot to tell you a dream I had Monday night."

"Good. I want to hear it."

"I can't believe I forgot to tell you, but today it was like the Lord reminded me, almost saying that I was responsible for telling you about it. Like He'd given it to me, and so I needed to share it with you."

"Okay, good. What was it?"

"Well, I was back in Mountain View. I guess I need to come back there," she said as we both chuckled. "You had your book in the car, and we drove past Mr. Grisham's house. As we did, we saw John walking into the house."

I turned down Dodd Mountain and continued to listen.

"'We have to stop and go in.' you said. You pulled your car over and put your book in your purse, and we walked up to the door together. They welcomed you in, so we went in and all the family was sitting in the living room in a circle. They could all see us as we stood there. We were introduced to everyone; then you turned to John and said, 'Can I talk with you a couple of minutes?'

'Me?' he said as he kinda laughed, 'Sure.'

So, you all stepped out of the room, and I was left in the living room with the family. After a few minutes you came back in to the room."

"And when I did, did I have the book, or did I give it to him?"

"No, you gave it to him."

"Was he happy or what?"

"Yeah, he was good."

"And then, I got up on a soapbox. I started to testify about what I've seen in your life. The miracles, signs, and visions, and then, I can see it so clearly. I remember I said this: 'And we are asking that this book be translated into all the languages your books are published in.'"

"Michelle, it's awesome," I stammered as I drove down Main street in a daze, almost unaware of why I'd even come to town.

"Then we left, and that was my dream. And I wondered if I'd had it because we'd talked that day, but it was like God said, 'No, I gave it for a reason; you need to tell her.'"

"I'm so glad you did. I needed to hear this. It's been a few weeks since I've heard anything, and God has brought you and my hairdresser with specific words today. I know He is bringing it forth. And you know, I'm studying Acts, and that is what these people are doing. Like Stephen. He doesn't just tell them Jesus is Lord; he starts at the beginning of the story, Abraham, Isaac, and Jacob. He testifies. I love that you testified."

"Yes, I did. And I remember those exact words about it being translated into many languages."

The next week I attempted to deliver the manuscript to John Grisham while he was with his family at church. My failure to do so was like being hit in the stomach. I couldn't figure out what God was doing, but I felt that I was obeying and that God would still bring it to pass.

One evening as I was praying, I grew even more certain of what God was about to do. Even more confident. I began to pray for the Lord to allow me to deliver the book on neutral ground. The following Monday morning in my prayer time, I heard in my spirit,

"The expectation of the righteous…"

I had just read Proverbs 10, and didn't recall reading any verse with those words, so I googled the phrase. Several verses came up, one of those being from Proverbs 10, except in a different version than my Bible which is why I didn't recall reading it that morning.

"The expectation of the righteous is joy," (Proverbs 10:28).[8]

"Expectation…"

---

[8] Fox, Michael V. *Proverbs 10-31: A New Translation with Introduction and Commentary.* Yale University Press, 2009. 527.

The word kept playing over and over in my mind. I knew what it meant, but I wanted to get a true definition of the word. So I looked it up. I found, "a belief that something will happen or is likely to happen; a feeling or belief about how successful, good, etc., someone or something will be..."[9]

Then I read a devotional about expecting from God. Standing on His promises and expecting that what He has promised He will carry out. I bowed my head to pray and immediately heard,

"Expect the delivery."

At that moment the Lord gave me a vision of two very important deliveries taking place in my life: the delivery of a child and the delivery of a timely word through the pages of my manuscript.

I got up feeling even more sure, even more expectant.

A store on the square in Mountain View where the t-shirt once hung, in this picture a decorative anchor

And later that day, as I was walking into the store with my kids, I quoted boldly, 'We have this hope as an anchor for the soul' (Hebrews 6:19, NIV), one that is sure, one that is steadfast, and one that holds within the veil. Right, kids?"

They nodded.

I walked a few more steps and noticed a young lady walking toward me wearing a shirt with an anchor and the same verse from Hebrews—in fact, it was a shirt I'd seen in a store

---

[9] "Expectation." *Merriam Webster.* www.Merriam-Webster.com.

window on our first trip to Mountain View. I stopped her and said, "I love your shirt; in fact, I think you're wearing it just for me."

Then, I continued to wait for God to move in power.

As I *expected the delivery.*

CHAPTER 27

August arrived, and one morning in my prayer time, I was praying for a meeting to again take place between John Grisham and me. A meeting in a public place on neutral ground where I could finally deliver my manuscript to him. The Lord whispered to my heart,

"Isaiah seven, verse three."

So, I picked up my Bible and turned to the passage and read:

"Then the Lord said to Isaiah, 'Go out now to meet Ahaz, you and your son Shear-jashub, at the end of the conduit of the upper pool, on the highway to the fuller's field...'" (NASB).

Thinking I might have misheard the Lord, I continued to the next verse which spoke of being calm and having no fear.

"Oh, that was probably the verse I was supposed to read."

But then I felt a caution in my heart.

"No, that is not the verse. It is Isaiah seven, verse three."

So, I read it again.

"Then the Lord said to Isaiah, 'Go out now to meet Ahaz, you and your son Shear-jashub, at the end of the conduit of the upper pool, on the highway to the fuller's field...'" (NASB).

Isaiah was going out to meet a king in a public place—a confirmation to what I had been praying for.

"Lord, you sent Isaiah out to meet King Ahaz, and You told him where to go. An upper pool, the highway, I'm sure all those places were fully public. Please let me meet him on neutral ground where I can speak with him and deliver this book."

I didn't know where that meeting would take place, but I also knew I never had to go out of my way to know about such things. God always showed me, and I trusted Him to do it again.

My mom and dad, my sister, Katherine, and Katherine's kids planned one last trip to see us before the summer ended. Our money continued to be tight, but there were a few things that needed to be replaced. Before they arrived, I dropped my phone in a creek. We didn't have the money to replace it, so the cell phone company was loaning me a flip phone, which I was actually starting to enjoy! The kids laughed at me when I pulled it out of my purse and flipped it open, but I was realizing how much time I spent looking at Facebook and the news, and being without the internet freed a lot of my time.

Our dryer had also gone out, and we didn't have the money to replace it, either. With a family of six, trips to the laundromat were a daily event. I was embarrassed when my family came, knowing I would also have to take their clothes to the laundromat, but I tried to save face. I told them that perhaps our landlord would fix it since she was the owner of the machine, even though we had not yet asked her. All I knew is if she said she wouldn't, we wouldn't be fixing it either.

One morning during their visit, my mom and I were standing in the kitchen making pancakes. She set the spatula down, turned to me, and said, "Rachel, I had a dream last night."

I swallowed hard, "What was it?"

"Well, I was in the house I grew up in. You know, it's funny, a lot of my dreams take place there. I guess it's because of childhood memories," she paused to stir the batter, "Anyway, I was sitting in a recliner in the living room, and I looked over and saw a man lying on the couch."

"Yeah?" I asked cautiously.

"He turned around to look at me—that's when I recognized who it was. It was John Grisham."

I turned to look at her, "And you recognized him?"

"Well, yeah. I've read a lot of his books."

"Okay, so then what?"

"So, all I could think about was the fact that I needed to get you over to the house right away. I wanted to tell him about the books I'd written, but I knew you'd get upset if I chased him away with my own stuff, so I decided to call you instead."

We both laughed.

"Thanks, Mom. That was nice of you."

"You arrived, and I answered the door. You came in and had your book in your hand, and you walked over to the couch. He sat up, and he looked at you and said, 'Hey, I remember you.'"

"Really? He remembered me?"

"Yeah, he remembered meeting you at church. So, he sat up and asked, 'What's that in your hands?' And you said, 'This is a book I've been working on.' Then he said, 'Can I read it?' and he reached his hand out for it. You gave it to him, and then I woke up. And that was it. That was the dream."

I looked intently into her eyes.

"Mom, that's awesome."

"Yeah, I thought it was pretty cool, too."

"I mean, have you ever had a dream with him in it? Even in these last months of me telling you my story?"

"No, never. That's why I thought it was so cool," she said, smiling as she and put a dollop of batter onto the pancake griddle, "Whatcha think about it?"

I paused as I thought a moment about it.

"Well, I've been praying for God to let me give it to him sometime out in public, on neutral ground, where no one can stop it. Maybe he'll even remember meeting me, who knows. How awesome, Mom. Thank you for sharing that with me."

And as I continued to help put breakfast on the table for the kids who were hungrily waiting, I was overwhelmed with how God was still enlisting people into the army that was marching the message forward.

My second appointment with my ob/gyn in Mountain Home was scheduled the day after my family left. The night before the appointment, Michael and I were talking after the kids were in bed.

"Remember months ago when someone told us John Grisham flies into Mountain Home then drives here?"

"Yeah, I do," he said.

"Wouldn't it be funny if I ran into him sometime up there with all these times I'll be going to the doctor?"

"Yeah, it would. I guess you never know."

As I was getting dressed for my appointment, I decided to print out the most recent copy of my book. When it was done, I placed it in a manila envelope and headed out the door. As I drove there, I wondered what I should do. But then I knew, too, that I never had to search it out; God always led me. He had faithfully led me every step of the way, and I knew He wouldn't stop now. Again, I was reminded of two very important deliveries taking place in my life: the delivery of a child and the delivery of this manuscript. I thought perhaps the Lord had led me to Mountain Home for both to take place.

My appointment was a quick check-up, so when I got out to the car, I called Michael, who had taken the kids to the library back at home.

"Well, I'm all done, so I guess I'll come on back."

"You should drive past the airport before you do."

"Really?" I said as I looked in the rearview mirror and backed up. "Well, I don't know. I don't even know where it is."

"I don't know, babe. I gotta go. I can't be on the phone in here."

We hung up as I turned onto the road that had led me to the hospital. I didn't have GPS on my flip phone, so I prayed, "Holy Spirit, lead me."

And then I drove.

I drove and drove for about ten miles. I was outside the city limits and entering another little town when I thought I'd go ahead and turn around at a gas station I was approaching.

"I'm gonna turn around at that Citgo."

But right before I did, I saw a sign for a business on my left. And attached to their sign was a large, iron anchor.

"Oh, God. It's from You," I thought as my pulse started to race.

And as I approached the gas station to turn around, I saw a second sign, "Baxter County Regional Airport," and it had an arrow pointing to the street that ran alongside the convenience store.

I turned the corner, and a mile later, I arrived at the airport. I drove through the parking lot and looked around before I turned back out onto the highway. There were a few planes, some parked cars, and a Subway restaurant. It was lunchtime, so I decided to go in for a sandwich. I placed my manuscript in my purse and headed into the restaurant.

As the employee was fixing my sandwich I asked, "So, everyone who comes in here…are they from the airport or from the town?"

"Ah, it's about a fifty-fifty split, half airport, half people off the highway."

"Oh, okay."

I sat down nervously to eat, and each time the door opened, my heart started to race.

"What would I say? I don't know. The Holy Spirit will give me the words," I thought with each creak of the hinges.

But after about thirty minutes, I was done and ready to leave.

"Lord, You'll arrange it at the right time. I thank You for leading me here," I thought as I threw my trash in the garbage and headed out to my car.

As I drove out to the main road, I passed a laundromat on the left-hand side.

"If I lived here, that's probably where I'd be hanging out right now," I laughed as I thought of the trip I needed to make to our own laundromat with two or three loads of clothes.

The next morning in my prayer time, I read the passage in Isaiah in different translations and read several more commentaries on it, as well. I read about Solomon's upper and lower pools. I read in depth about the conversation between King Ahaz and Isaiah. I thought about the fact that Isaiah took his son, and wondered if I, too, was taking a son with me on each trip to Mountain Home. Then, I read the passage in the NIV version, "Then the Lord said to Isaiah, 'Go out, you and your son Shear-Jashub, to meet Ahaz at the end of the aqueduct of the Upper Pool, on the road to the Launderer's Field'" (Isaiah 7:3, NIV).

That afternoon, when I started the next chapter in my book explaining the story, it hit me as I typed out the verse—the laundromat was next to the airport.

"Oh my gosh. The phrase 'On the road to the Launderer's Field,' spoke clearly and sharply to my heart. "Yes, the airport is on the road to the Launderer's Field."

Camille came to me and asked about my appointment and where else I'd gone in Mountain Home. I told her I'd eaten lunch at Subway and was reminded of the prophetic words spoken to me by the preacher in Branson, "When you hear the train coming, know that it is coming for you."

A month later on my way to the doctor's office again, I placed my manuscript in the car and planned a lunch trip to the airport afterwards. In my prayer time that morning, I'd asked the Lord to put His "stamp of approval" on my story and on the location I'd believed He had shown me.

"Father, will You confirm this location by confirming the verse You gave me? Let me find out today that I am, in fact, carrying a son?"

After waiting about thirty minutes, the nurse called me back.

"Good morning, Rachel. How are you? Today we will do your twenty week ultrasound first; then you will see the doctor."

"Okay," I said as I walked down the hall to the dimly-lit room.

I stepped inside, set my purse down, and climbed onto the exam table.

"We'll look at the heart, the brain, the length of the bones in the thighs…things like that; then if you'd like to know the sex of the baby, and if he or she cooperates, I can let you know. Do you want to find out?"

"Yes, please," I said as I pulled my skirt down past my belly.

She squeezed the warm jelly onto my abdomen and pulled out the ultrasound machine. As she placed the scope on me and moved it around I asked, "Everything look okay?"

"Oh, yes. Looks great. The baby is very active."

She measured the baby, measured the bones, looked for all valves of the heart, looked for a cleft lip, studied the brain, and checked the heart rate. After about five minutes, she said, "Okay everything looks great. Ready to find out what you're having?"

"Yes!"

"Okay," she moved the machine to a different location, "now you're seeing the underside of the baby's body and between the legs. Can you see that?"

"Yes."

"Okay, well, it's a boy!"

"Oh, that's great news! My son has prayed for months for a baby brother, and the Lord is answering His prayers."

"Yes, He is. You can tell your son that his prayers were answered," she smiled.

When I was finished, I drove toward the airport, paying special attention to the signs God had given. I slowed down as I passed the anchor and smiled. Sitting directly across from the airport was a water tower.

"Oh," I paused to catch my breath, "Could that be symbolic of an aqueduct? God, the further You bring me into this story, the more I want to take my shoes off and step back. It is so holy."

It was like I could step back and look at this book as something I had not done but rather something He and He alone had done. I was so enamored with all the confirmations of the day that I went into Subway, ate quickly, and left quickly. I wanted to get home quickly to tell my family the good news of a baby brother. I couldn't wait!

CHAPTER 28

As the days continued to pass, I'd occasionally wrestle with doubt. I was amazed at where God had brought me in my journey. But I'd wonder when the end result would come or *if* it would come. I knew some people thought I was crazy, but then I'd go right back to leaning on God and believing everything He'd said. I was only allowing a few, intimate friends to know the details of my story so they would stand in faith with me. Others, I knew, didn't need to know what the Lord was leading me to do. It kept my army sharp, swift, and wise.

A month later at my next check-up, I decided to run some errands before going to Subway for lunch. Around noon, after I'd picked up a few early Christmas gifts for the kids, I drove towards the airport.

"Alright, Lord, if today is the day I deliver this book, then align me. Give me the words to say. I pray I wouldn't speak on my own but only speak what the Holy Spirit wants me to speak."

I grew more and more nervous the closer I got to the airport. My heart started beating faster and faster.

"Okay, it's now or never. If he's in there, Lord, tell me what to say."

I reached over to the passenger seat and grabbed my purse which held the manuscript. Walking toward the Subway door, I took a deep breath as I clutched it a little closer to my side. When I reached the door, I pulled the handle toward me. And it pulled back. I tried again. And it was still stuck.

"What in the world?" I thought as I leaned in closer to see why the door was locked.

I peered into the restaurant.

I was shocked.

It was empty.

"What? How can that be?"

I continued looking through the glass. All the tables were gone, the signs, the chairs; everything was gone. The only remaining equipment was the drink machine.

"Am I dreaming?"

I felt like I'd been hit in the stomach.

In awe, I walked back to my car, got in, and sat there in amazement.

I didn't even know what to pray, so I called Michael.

"Hello?"

"Just when you thought my story couldn't get any crazier, it did."

"What?"

"Well, I came to Subway, because He's led me here...I walk up to the door, with my book in hand, pull the door, and it's locked. At first I think, well it's closed, but as I look through the window, I see everything is gone. The Subway restaurant, where

I thought God led me, is now out of business. I don't know whether to laugh or cry."

"No way. Are you serious?"

"Yes! I mean, come on God, what are you doing to me? Leading me on a wild goose chase? What is He doing?"

"Man, babe, I'm sorry."

We sat a moment in silence.

"I know this all looks crazy, but I am certain God's led me here, otherwise I'd not be doing this, you know?"

"Yeah, I know. You've been obedient."

Silence.

"You know, Rachel, do you ever wonder if God is seeing how far you'll follow Him? How obedient you'll be? No matter what He's asked you to do, you've done it. It's like He's saying, 'Yes, I can trust Rachel; she's obeying.'" He paused then asked, "You have your Bible with you, right?"

"Yeah."

"And your journal?"

"Yeah."

"Well, sit there. Turn on the air, sit there, and wait on Him. Don't leave until you make a phone call or wait for an e-mail to come or something. He's going to give you your next step. He always does. Sit there in the parking lot until He speaks to you."

"Yeah, okay, I guess so. I guess I'll do that."

"We're okay here. Take your time and wait for Him to show you."

"Okay, I'll do that."

I decided to take Michael's advice. I got in the car and turned on the air conditioner. It was, after all, an unusually hot fall afternoon. I took my Bible and my journal from the passenger seat and set it in my lap. Then I closed my eyes, "Lord, I'm not mad at You. I've come to know You better than that. Each time I've hit a brick wall, You've only redirected me. You've never let me lay this story down without picking it back up. Lord, I trust You will do something even more miraculous."

Then tenderly yet powerfully, I heard,

"Isaiah 49:11."

I turned the pages and read, "I will make all My mountains a road, and My highways will be raised up" (NASB).

Then again, in my heart, I heard,

"Isaiah 11:3."

So, I turned to it as well and read, "And He will delight in the fear of the Lord, And He will not judge by what His eyes see, Nor make a decision by what His ears hear" (NASB).

The pilot in front of me was now taxiing down to the runway. I sat and watched. Thinking about how a dead end was never a dead end with God.

I waited.

I quickly turned back to Isaiah 49:11

". . .And my highways will be raised up" (NASB).

The plane was now taking off into the sky. I pulled my hair back, twisted it up onto my head, and rested my hands there. The plane left the concrete and pavement and rose onto a road made of air and tailwinds, and I drove home.

After dinner, I decided to take the kids to the park. When I did, I called Michelle and told her how the day had unfolded.

"When you went back into your car, did God say anything?"

"Yeah, He said He was going to raise the highway, and I'm still praying about that."

"Okay, good."

"Michelle, each step I take requires more and more faith. You're still with me, right? You're still supporting me in this, aren't you?" I said as I pushed Mary Manor on the swing.

"Oh yeah, I am! I'm on this raft with you until the end. If it sinks, we are going down together," she said as we both laughed.

"Honestly, Rachel, let me say this. I do not believe the Lord has put John Grisham in the position he's in for John's self-gratification. He's put John Grisham in that position for His glory."

We sat a moment in silence.

"Yeah, you're right."

"Let me pray for you; then I gotta go put kids in bed."

Then she prayed the most beautiful prayer. She prayed something so specific, so relevant for Michael, "And God, I pray for Michael. Lord, I pray that he would no longer have to exhaust himself with his work and providing for his family, but that You would put the apple directly in front of him. That he would not have to reach and climb to get it, but that you would put it right in front of him with ease. It would be his for the taking."

That night, after the kids were in bed, Michael and I sat on our bed and laughed at the events of the day.

"Yep, there I was, standing in front of the Subway, wondering where it had gone! I mean, who does that happen to, except me?"

I collapsed on the bed next to him.

"So what now?" he said has he put the pillow under his arms.

I opened my Bible and read him the verse God had given me. I told him maybe God would somehow let me fly the book to the airport.

"And I know how ridiculous it sounds, but I don't know. It's the verse that came to mind."

"Yeah, it seems crazy, but let's just see what God does…"

The next day, Michael decided to visit area schools in hopes of booking presentations using my books and his performance skills. He'd presented at several schools in Tennessee, and he was going to see if he'd have favor in Arkansas schools.

Within three days, Michael had booked eight schools. Every school he visited either said yes or to check back within a few days to see if they could schedule a visit. He received no "nos."

While Michael was out visiting schools and the kids were doing schoolwork, I was reading the Bible study book I'd been studying for two months, *Discerning the Voice of God* by Priscilla Shirer, when two paragraphs completely jumped off the page at me:

"When airplanes land, their individual flight pattern is not all that matters. The air-traffic controller must consider all the planes in the air and on the ground. When the pilot receives the next instruction depends on all those planes. If a pilot says, 'I'm going to land' before receiving instructions from the tower, the results can be disastrous to him and many other people."[10]

A tingle ran up my spine.

Then, the study asked:

"How does this analogy apply to waiting on instructions from the Father?"

To which I wrote:

"I feel I've waited ten years for instructions, and now I am receiving them step by step. I must follow them faithfully."

The next paragraph read:

"Pilots must learn to wait for directions from someone with a greater perspective. When pilots do receive instructions, they only do as much as they have been instructed to do. Then they wait for more instructions. Each step and the timing of these

---

[10] Shirer, Priscilla. *Discerning the Voice of God*. Workbook. Moody Publishers, 2012.

instructions is crucial to the success of all involved. When God gives you instructions, trust that He has given you what you need for now. He will give more when the time is right."[11]

"God, how personal for me! Thank you for confirming your words to me!"

Two weeks later, Michael had booked twenty-one school presentations and one Christmas show. It was a record. He'd never booked so many shows at one time. Truly, it was plucking the apple that was growing right in front of him.

---

[11] Ibid.

CHAPTER 29

I was making breakfast when my mom called. "I want to tell you about the party we went to last night for Burt Thomas," she said.

"Oh, what a blast from the past! How're they?"

"Good. You know, he turned eighty this week, and they had a surprise party for him."

"Well, how fun! Gosh, when is the last time you've seen them?"

"Oh, it's been at least fifteen to twenty years," she shared, "but this is so cool. Let me tell you. His daughter-in-law came over—she remembered me from years ago, and we started talking. I told her about Katherine and about you. I told her you lived in Arkansas with your family, and she said she lived in Arkansas, too. Guess where?"

"Where?" I asked as I put the plates in the sink.

"Mountain Home."

"No way."

"Yeah. You remember Burt and Linda's son, Kelley?"

"Vaguely."

"Anyway, they own a nursery in Mountain Home. I told her that is where your ob/gyn is, but I couldn't remember his name."

I pulled a towel out of the drawer and turned around slowly.

"Wait, Kelley Thomas, right?"

"Yeah, Kelley Thomas. Remember? He always worked in nursery stuff, trees, plants, all that. Well, he moved from Texas to Mountain Home and opened his business there."

"Mom, you're not going to believe this. I know exactly where it is."

"You do?"

"Yeah, I do. It's on the same highway as the hospital, the airport, and the anchor, all the stuff God has shown me in His Word and through prophetic words—yep, I know exactly where it is. In fact, the first time I drove to the airport, I noticed it because it said 'Kelley,' and I noticed it was spelled the same way as my name."

"Well, who knows," she paused on the other end of the line, "maybe God did it just for you."

Later when I told Michelle the story, she said, "Look at it like this, Rachel, you are on the right road."

CHAPTER 30

Michael took the kids and visited a different church as I was really tired and decided to stay home and rest. It was a church we'd visited before, so they knew Michael and knew he entertained. After they returned, he said, "They wanted me to sing tonight, but I told them I didn't want to do that right now," he said as he pulled out a chair at the table and sat down. "I told them I needed prayer, so the pastor circled up some people around me, and they prayed. And it was pretty powerful."

"I bet."

"Even Caroline, when they were done, was like, 'Dad, that was powerful.'"

I nodded my head. "So, did anyone give you a prophetic word?"

"Yes, and guess what it was?"

"No, just tell me!" I said laughingly as I sat down at the table across from him.

"When the pastor was finished, he said, 'Michael, God is your anchor.'"

"What? No way!"

"Yes he did. Then he goes, 'Your anchor is sure and steadfast and holds within the veil.'"

"Oh my gosh! I love it!"

"A few minutes after that, one of the men who prayed got up and sang a song about anchors."

"Don't you think that's awesome? God's still saying what He's said all along. The anchor holds."

The next day, we were scheduled to speak at the church where Michael and the kids had visited. He decided to sing a few songs then share what had happened over the weekend. He told me he wanted to be transparent and tell them what he was going through, not perform his usual comedy routine. So, he did. Then, I stood up when he was finished and shared what I'd learned from the experience. When we were finished sharing, I told the congregation that we'd be happy to meet with anyone who wanted prayer.

To my surprise, the first couple to come forward was the pastor and his wife! He told the members that they needed prayers for their health and for God's will in their lives.

It was a new experience for Michael and me.

I guess I didn't know what to expect when we stood before the people and asked them to come forward.

They came.

After we finished bowing our heads, laying our hands on the pastor and his wife, and praying, I opened my eyes to a host of people standing around us.

"Oh, what do I do now?"

The pastor had handed us a small vial of oil, so I held it in my hands and nudged Michael as to ask what we were supposed to do.

"Should we pray for everyone at once? Or one by one?"

There seemed to be so many of them, and only Michael and I stood there to receive them. So, the pastor came and stood with us and began to tell us each of their stories. He prayed for the first two as I tried to wrap my head around what I should be doing. Then, I relaxed, put the oil on my fingertips, anointed them one at a time, and prayed right alongside Michael.

The next day as I was driving to pick up Micah and Camille from basketball, I asked the Lord to give me a word for John Grisham. I didn't want this to seem like just another person trying to get a book into his hands, like I'm sure had happened a million times before.

"God, what can I say to him? Give me a word," I prayed as I stopped at the stoplight. I stared at the sky as the sun was setting behind the hills.

Then softly, sweetly in my spirit I heard,

"Tell him it is time to turn the spotlight on Me."

I continued to look at the clouds as they turned to pink and orange.

"Okay, Lord, what else?"

"It's time for him to tell the world about whom he loves and serves."

Our family had decided to attend a different church in town. We needed some distance and clarity and were all in agreement that new surroundings would be good for us. One night while walking, I was thinking about a conversation we'd had in Sunday School. Our baby boy was due in late January, and the first time I met with the nurse at the doctor's office, I asked her how difficult it was for people to get from Mountain View to Mountain Home in the winter.

"Well, it can go either way."

"Ice or no ice, right?"

"It can be nice weather, and you'll have no trouble, or you can ice skate all the way here."

"So, do you know of ladies who don't make it here to deliver?"

"Sometimes."

The conversation replayed in my mind. I had thought of it often. I'd asked for several phone numbers from people I knew were more familiar with driving on icy roads in the mountains than Michael and I were. My family was nervous for me, my mom especially, who asked on a regular basis if I was going to be induced or who was going to drive me or what would I do if we couldn't get to the hospital. None of the questions I could answer, except that God was in charge and I trusted Him.

"If Michael is on a cruise ship," I said to our Sunday School friends, "I'll drive myself to the hospital, have this baby, and drive home myself. Michael can FaceTime me from the Bahamas," I laughed as I sat next to Michael, knowing there was a chance I'd be giving birth without him present.

"You can call any one of us, and we'll come help out," the class said laughingly while sharing phone numbers.

185

"Actually, the Merricks have a plane if you need to be flown to Mountain Home."

"Really?" I asked.

"Sure, we can fly you up to be delivered if we're snowed in."

"It would be interesting, wouldn't it? If I went into labor and had to get to Mountain Home on a plane?" I answered.

Before I went to bed, I jotted down my thoughts on the subject in my journal and then wrote: "Lord, pull me into your plan."

A snow and ice storm came through Arkansas the night before my 39-weeks appointment. There were so many things on my mind—the baby, the book, Michael's travels, and going into labor while being an hour away. I knew my blood pressure must've been creeping up higher and higher. I picked up my Bible and opened it to the Psalm 37:

> Do not fret because of evildoers,
> Be not envious toward wrongdoers.
> For they will wither quickly like the grass
> And fade like the green herb.
> Trust in the LORD and do good;
> Dwell in the land and cultivate faithfulness.
> Delight yourself in the LORD;
> And He will give you the desires of your heart.
> Commit your way to the LORD,
> Trust also in Him, and He will do it.
> He will bring forth your righteousness as the light
> And your judgment as the noonday.
> Rest in the LORD and wait patiently for Him (Psalms
37:1-7a, NASB).

Rest and wait seemed to be exactly what the Lord was speaking to my heart.

After I left, I decided to drive past the airport one last time to pray. I pulled up outside the chain link fence, opened my Bible to Joel 2, and read:

> Then I will make up to you for the years
> That the swarming locust has eaten,
> The creeping locust, the stripping locust and the
> gnawing locust,
> My great army which I sent among you.
> You will have plenty to eat and be satisfied
> And praise the name of the LORD your God,
> Who has dealt wondrously with you;
> Then My people will never be put to shame.
> Thus you will know that I am in the midst of Israel,
> And that I am the LORD your God,
> And there is no other;
> And My people will never be put to shame.
>
> It will come about after this
> That I will pour out My Spirit on all mankind;
> And your sons and daughters will prophesy,
> Your old men will dream dreams,
> Your young men will see visions.
> Even on the male and female servants
> I will pour out My Spirit in those days (Joel 2:25-29,
> NASB).

Closing my Bible, I opened the door and stepped out. Walking over to the fence, I took out my anointing oil and watched the drops hit the grass.

"Lord, let it be so," I said as I placed my hands on the cold metal. "Not for me, but for Your glory. Let your Word go forth from this place. Get this book over this fence, I pray."

I placed the lid back on the bottle, got inside the car, and drove home to Mountain View.

After I got home, Michael and I talked about the possibility of me going into labor and him being on the ship, so I called Michelle.

"It's so much to think about. I didn't think I'd go into labor this early, and now Michael is leaving in two days. I'm overwhelmed."

"Hey, just say the word. We're planning on comin' in the next week or two anyway to help, so if you'd rather me come this weekend, I'll come."

"Okay, yeah, that might be a good idea, so I won't be alone."

Before Michael left, I went ahead and scheduled an induction for when he returned the following week.

CHAPTER 31

One morning I was thinking about a certain time when we lived in Tennessee. Earlier in our marriage, I began to see images and visions in my mind that I believed to be from God. I didn't know if it was a way the Lord had always spoken to me and I hadn't recognized it or if it was a new work He was doing. But when they came, they were clear and comforting.

When the tide started to turn and I began to see the extreme lengths God was using to speak to me, I became more aware of the visions. I remember one morning, years earlier, when I'd thought about fireworks during my quiet time. I could see them, like a grand finale and even looked up a fireworks show on YouTube before we left for church to watch one. That morning, I asked the Lord, "I'd like to see a fireworks show today. I know You can do it, and I ask that You will do it today. I want to know You're still in this situation."

It was a cold, winter morning, and I didn't know how it would happen, but I asked for it. That afternoon, I took the kids to a movie at the local Pulaski theater. I was passing down popcorn to everyone when I heard several pops and bangs coming from the screen. By the time I looked up, the scene was over. Leaning over, I asked Caroline, "What did I miss?"

"Oh, it was some fireworks."

I was so frustrated! I'd asked God for a fireworks show, He had delivered, but I was too busy passing out food to see it! I sat there the next hour of the movie wondering what I could do to see the opening scene again.

"Maybe I can ask them to restart the film before we leave, so I can see it. I'll tell them I missed the first part and ask if I can stay to watch it again." Then a little later, I thought, "Nah, God's big enough. I've asked to see fireworks today, and He's big enough to show me. I'm not gonna do anything but sit here and trust Him to do it."

He answered my prayers when, during the last scene of the film, a huge fireworks display erupted. My faith increased. Knowing I could ask. Knowing I could wait on Him, do nothing, but trust Him with even the smallest of requests. God didn't answer this way every time I asked for something, but when things like this happened, I knew He alone had done it.

Fireworks became a symbol for me during the years that followed, and often I'd referred to my year and a half living in Mountain View as a fireworks show because of all the miracles on display; they just kept on coming!

When Michelle and her kids arrived, I was so glad to see them. While the kids played, we visited and cooked dinner, and later we eventually got everyone in bed. We hadn't mentioned the book that evening, and the next morning we were up getting coffee in the kitchen and getting ready for church when Michelle turned to me and said, "I've got to tell you what happened last night."

"Okay," I said as I poured cream into my cup.

"So, you know Whitney has a big meeting tonight at the church, and I was up praying for him. I don't know what's gonna take place, but I started praying."

She'd told me the night before that her husband, who pastored a church in Cookeville, Tennessee, was having a meeting with several high-up officials in their church. I imagined they were both anxious as to why the meeting was called, so I was not surprised to know she'd been up praying.

"I was lying in bed, praying and praying, not able to get it off my mind. Asking God to take care of it, whatever it was, and to give Whitney peace, you know. So, as I was praying, I started seeing flashing lights. Immediately, I thought 'caution,'" so I started interceding more specifically."

"You saw flashing lights, in the room?"

"No, like a vision. I saw these flashing lights on the ground."

She took a drink from her mug as I leaned up against the kitchen counter, and then she continued, "A few minutes later, I paused, and then one of the flashing lights shot straight up," she said. "It was a firework."

"Really?" I asked as I sank back onto the counter a little more.

"And I kept watching, and boom, boom, boom, the sky was full of fireworks."

As her words left her mouth, I wondered if the vision was for me as I felt the sting of a tear in my eye.

"My feeling went from caution to jubilation, like this was time to celebrate, but I wasn't quite sure what was being celebrated. I asked God to show me, to open my eyes, but then I fell asleep. Then, it must've been four of five in the morning when I woke up again, and the vision was immediately on my heart. I prayed for God to show me, and instantly I knew it was for you."

I reached up and wiped my eyes with the collar of my robe.

"I asked Him if I was to share it with you, and immediately I saw the skyline of Mountain View. Like the view from your front porch. And the entire skyline was lit up. Just as clear as I'd seen the fireworks, I was now seeing this valley surrounded by mountains that were illuminated. I was definitely supposed to share it with you. It was for you."

"Oh, Michelle. You know how God's used those in my life."

"Yes, I know. Remember last year, when we got down on our faces and laid hands on your book, right in the living room?"

"Yes! Yes!"

"I remember praying and saying that God was bringing it all together, like a fireworks finale, one miracle after another."

"Yes, I know! I remember that!" I said as I continued to wipe the tears that were falling down my cheeks.

"Well, that vision I had last night was like I was overcome with the Spirit. I'm tellin' you, I haven't been that immersed in the Spirit in a long time."

Michelle left, Michael returned, and I waited. My heart became restless when I tried to figure it all out—devise a plan, think of a route, map out my own way. I'd get worn out and the weight seemed burdensome. I could not bring His thoughts down to my own—no. They were much higher than mine (Isaiah 55:8-9). I felt a heaviness bearing down on me, so I prayed, waited, and listened. I was too worried about everything going on. If there was any verse that had spoken to me for many years it was, "Unless the Lord builds the house, the builders labor in vain" (Psalm 127:1, NIV). Oh, how I had played that verse over and over in my mind. Maybe after ten years, it was starting to make more sense to me. I knew if God was going to do a work through me, it would be God, not me. And that is where I had to live in my faith. I thought of the verse, "Without faith it is impossible to please God..." (Hebrews 11:6, NIV), and rested on the fact that God would make a way. God would stay true to His promises. God and only God would deliver me. But, I had to continue to have faith. I had to continue to anchor in. I had to totally trust Him to bring about what He had told me He would.

So, I gave it over to Him.

When worry crept back in, I went back to what I knew. While I was writing in my journal, I had an overwhelming peace about giving everything over to God. In fact, I wrote, "I resolve to do nothing. I've been given no further marching orders, so until that time, I resolve to do nothing but rest and wait." Then, I signed and dated it, "Rachel Kelley 1/31/16."

CHAPTER 32

I gave birth to my precious son Christopher on February 4th, 2016. I was induced so Michael would be able to attend, and

Christopher's first Sunday at church

we were so grateful. Michael left the next day for the ship. After arriving home from the hospital, I was happy, healthy, and enjoying holding my sweet baby boy, Christopher. Michael was on a ship, I was recuperating, and my mom and dad were on their way to help. My schedule slowed down, and I rested. In that time, I was reminded that the Lord said He "…gently leads those that have young" (Isaiah 40:11, NIV).

Then, the peace came.

Spring arrived, and Michael and I were anxious to go on a date night alone—well, alone with only the baby! Dane and Heather had given us tickets to a concert in town. The concert began, and we enjoyed clapping along while listening to the Gaelic music. I noticed a few ladies sitting in front of us, and as one turned, I saw a pentagram necklace, an emblem typically associated with witchcraft and the occult.

Intermission arrived, and I got up to use the restroom. As I was walking back to my seat, the woman with the necklace was walking toward me. She was hobbling on a cane and seemed to be having a difficult time walking up the slope to the restroom. When we passed in the aisle, I smiled and moved over to allow her cane plenty of room. Suddenly, I heard,

"You are going to lay your hands on her knees and pray for her to be healed."

Turning into the aisle, I moved toward my seat.

"That's not what I just heard, is it?"

I sat down next to Michael and debated the instructions I believed the Holy Spirit had given to me. I folded my arms across my chest then unfolded them.

"Oh no, Lord. That's way too awkward."

The musicians walked back out onto the stage, and I decided I was going to relax and enjoy my date. But no matter how much I tried to forget the thought throughout the remainder of the performance, I could not get it out of my mind. My hair felt heavy and damp on the back of my neck—I wiped my hands on my freshly pressed skirt.

There was no way to get around it. So, I started bargaining with the Lord.

"Ok, Lord. I'll do it," I relented. "I'll do it as long as she is outside by her car when we leave." Immediately, I saw a vision of her standing between our two cars. "Okay, Lord, if she is standing there when we leave, I'll pray for her."

The concert was coming to an end, applause arose from the crowd, and we started to stand up. The ladies in front of me turned around. I smiled, said hello, and waited for Michael to grab his coat.

195

"Okay, Lord, if she is standing out by the car, where I believe You have shown me she will be, I'll lay my hands on her knees and pray for her."

We were sharing a few laughs with some friends we ran into when the man behind us started asking Michael about his show. "By the time I get out of here, they'll be long gone," I thought as I had seen the ladies already walk out the back, "I'm off the hook."

We turned and walked toward the exit. Opening the large wooden door, I noticed the dark sky and bleakness of the night except where the parking lot lights were shining. I heard the sound of my heels on the rocky pebbles.

Crunching. Scraping.

Picking up speed, I turned toward our car while carrying Christopher in his car seat.

That's when I saw exactly what God had shown me.

The lady with the necklace was still there…standing exactly where I knew she'd be…in between our cars.

"Oh, Mighty Rushing Wind…I'm all in."

She turned to walk to the other side of her car.

Each crunch of my heel on the gravel lot took me closer to the woman and further from myself.

My hands started to shake. I shifted my grip on the handle of the car seat and turned toward Michael who was walking a few steps behind me.

"Listen, the Lord told me to pray for this woman, okay?"

Getting closer to the car, I cleared my throat. "That was a great show, wasn't it?"

The ladies turned and looked at me, "Oh, yeah, it was good. This is the fourth or fifth time we've come to hear them," said the one now standing by my side of the car.

"Yeah? Well, good!" I pulled the automatic latch on our van door and waited as it slid open. Placing Christopher inside, I cut my eyes over to see them opening their doors.

"This is it. It's now or never." I closed the baby's door.

The lady standing directly behind me turned to watch me put him in.

"Oh, he's so sweet. How old is he?"

"Just a few weeks…"

"Well, congratulations."

She turned around to face her car, "Have a good night."

I turned around, placed my hand on her shoulder and said, "Can you tell me the name of your friend?"

"Uh, yeah, it's Meagan."

Meagan was already seated in the car with her cane tucked underneath the seat.

"Do you think she'd mind if I laid my hands on her knees and prayed for God to heal her?"

"Uh, no. I don't think she'd mind that."

"Look, I'm sure it sounds odd, but I think it's what the Lord told me to do."

She continued to stand next to the door, so I decided to get in the driver's seat myself. I placed one hand on the steering wheel while I turned and stuck out my other hand. "Hi, Meagan. I'm Rachel."

"Nice to meet you."

"You'll probably think this is crazy, but when I saw you walking toward the restroom tonight, I felt the Lord tell me to place my hands on your knees and pray for healing for you."

"Oh, okay. Um, yeah, sure," she smiled as she seemed to warm up to the idea, "I'd appreciate it."

"Okay, tell me which knee is bothering you."

"This one," she pointed to the one on the left, "they've both been hurting for a few months, but this one's getting worse."

"Okay. Well, I'd like to pray for you, if that's alright. I'm out of my comfort zone," I laughed nervously and took my hand from the wheel and placed it in my lap, "but, crazy as it may seem, the Lord showed me where you'd be standing after the concert."

Then, I placed both my hands on her knees and took a deep breath. Then I prayed. I thanked God for her, for the plan He had for her life, and for the love He had for her. I prayed healing for her knees in Jesus's name. When I finished, I gave her a hug and said, "Well, I love you, Meagan, and so does the Lord. He has a great plan for you. I'm going to keep praying and believing for a complete healing."

"Thank you. I love you, too." She resituated herself in the seat. "Thank you for that."

"Absolutely. Thank the Lord for it."

I got out of the car and turned to the other woman who had been listening and agreeing with us. "What's your name?"

"Amanda."

I hugged her, too.

"God loves you, and He has a great plan for you. Thanks for letting me pray for your friend tonight."

"Thank you for doing it."

I moved so she could get in, opened up my car door, and sat down in the seat. I glanced over at Michael who was staring at me. "What was that all about?"

"God. He told me to do it," I said as I placed my purse on the floorboard and pulled the seatbelt across my chest.

He just smiled and backed out of the gravel lot.

CHAPTER 33

While visiting with a friend one day over lunch, we
started talking about the baptism of the Holy Spirit. She believed
that, in a Christian's life, the baptism of the Holy Spirit was a
separate event from accepting Christ as Savior and being water-
baptized. Being raised in a Charismatic church, I, too, was taught
about the baptism of the Holy Spirit as a separate event. But
honestly, I didn't know what I believed now that I was an adult.
All I knew was that God was doing something amazing in my
life...like an outpouring of the Holy Spirit. A new work. Like I'd
been standing knee-deep, wading in the water, and God had
pulled me under as the water was flowing over me. I couldn't
explain it, but I could almost pin-point it to the night I was
watching the *Costa Concordia* being raised out of the water.
Whatever God had done in my life at that point seemed to be
growing and consuming any unbelief within me.

"A new work..." is what my friend had said, but all I
knew was that it was overwhelming and powerful. And I wanted
Michael to have it, too.

I began to research the baptism of the Holy Spirit. I
wanted to know what God said about it, not what different
denominations thought about it. And I wanted to know more
about the gifts of the Holy Spirit. I found this passage in 1
Corinthians 12:4-11:

There are different kinds of gifts, but the same Spirit distributes them. There are different kinds of service, but the same Lord. There are different kinds of working, but in all of them and in everyone it is the same God at work.

Now to each one the manifestation of the Spirit is given for the common good. To one there is given through the Spirit a message of wisdom, to another a message of knowledge by means of the same Spirit, to another faith by the same Spirit, to another gifts of healing by that one Spirit, to another miraculous powers, to another prophecy, to another distinguishing between spirits, to another speaking in different kinds of tongues, and to still another the interpretation of tongues. All these are the work of one and the same Spirit, and he distributes them to each one, just as he determines (NIV).

Healing, prophecy, tongues...it seemed that some churches were not preaching this aspect of the Holy Spirit. But I knew it was truth. I had *experienced* it. And there was no denying that. Was speaking in tongues dead as some thought? What about visions and dreams? I knew it wasn't. I knew they weren't.

I wasn't questioning whether you could be a Christian and not speak in tongues or whether everyone should be prophesying and laying their hands on others to see them healed. It wasn't that at all. Rather, I was coming to know the Holy Spirit like I'd never known Him before. And He was so much more than I ever knew! He was Fire! How I hoped Christians would see and believe that the Holy Spirit could birth these powerful gifts in their lives. I thought about how much more effective we would be. As I continued to dig, I read 1 Corinthians 14:1-5:

Follow the way of love and eagerly desire gifts of the Spirit, especially prophecy. For anyone who speaks in a tongue does not speak to people but to God. Indeed, no one understands them; they utter mysteries by the Spirit. But the one who prophesies speaks to people for their strengthening, encouraging and comfort. Anyone who speaks in a tongue edifies themselves, but the one who prophesies edifies the church. I would like every one of you to speak in tongues, but I would rather have you prophesy. The one who prophesies is greater than the one who speaks in tongues, unless someone interprets, so that the church may be edified (NIV).

I began to pray that Michael would seek the baptism of the Holy Spirit. Or a complete immersion. Whatever the experience is called didn't matter to me—I prayed a filling up and an overflow of God's holy power for my husband.

Michael was scheduled to perform at the local General Baptist Church for their Homecoming. When the day arrived, we got the kids dressed and to church before the service began. I sat on the second row, right behind the pastor's wife. After a lively southern gospel praise service, the pastor got up at the podium. "If you have a need, I'd like you to come down for prayer."

"If you have a need?" I thought as I smiled. "I have lots of them."

I walked down the aisle of the small church along with about 90 % of the congregation when the pastor came up to me and touched my forehead. Surprisingly, I heard him praying in tongues.

"At a Baptist church?"

Then he began to pray for me, "Lord, bless this prophetess, I pray."

"Prophetess."

The words fell on me with a thud. It was as if he was confirming a gift that the Holy Spirit had already given to me. Confirming it and declaring it.

I started to go back to my seat, but Christopher was crying and needed to be fed, so I walked out the back of the sanctuary and down the hall to a Sunday school classroom. As I turned toward the teacher's table, I noticed a stack of books. *Speaking in Tongues* was on top. I picked it up, turned it over, and saw that it was written by a Baptist preacher. I sat down in the folding chair on the front row and thumbed through the pages.

"If Michael would read about speaking in tongues, it would be from a Baptist minister," I thought, astonished by the timing of it all.

I tucked it into my purse and told myself I'd ask the pastor if I could have it, but I ended up having to leave early because Christopher desperately needed a nap. So, away I went with it. That night as I sat across the couch from Michael, I told him what Pastor Kerry had said to me while praying. Then, I pulled out the book and placed it in his lap.

"Check this out sometime. I think you'll like it."

I sent a message to Pastor Kerry telling him I had borrowed the book that was in the Sunday school class, but he assured me I could keep it!

When Michael was asked to come to a local church to entertain the following weekend, I'd also been asked to come and share my story. We were at the park with the kids, and it was getting dark. I turned to Michael, "About the show this Sunday night. I'm kinda nervous."

"About what?"

"Well, we have some friends who go there, and some of them have read my blog, I'm sure. I guess I'm nervous about talking about the dreams and visions to a group who may not be familiar with that stuff."

"That reminds me…" he paused and pushed the swing that Christopher was in.

"What?" I asked.

"I didn't want to tell you this, but the pastor from the church where we are speaking in a couple of weeks doesn't want you talking about visions."

"Doesn't want me to talk about visions? Why?"

"Well, he said that they don't believe God operates that way today, and he asked me to tell you to not refer to that part of your story."

"Doesn't believe the Holy Spirit gives visions?" I could feel my face getting warm.

"I'm just telling you what he said."

"But, that's a lot of my story, and you know it. A lot of what I've learned recently is the supernatural part of God. And they want me to not speak about it?"

"I knew you were going to be upset."

"That's what's wrong with some churches today. They want to shut down the Holy Spirit. But that's what the world needs to see. There is a power so much greater than what we know, and we don't need to stifle it."

When Michael came home from the theater that weekend, he'd brought us ice cream to share.

"Guess who I saw in the ice cream aisle?"

"Who?"

"Pastor Kerry from General Baptist."

"Yeah, what'd he say?"

"He said a lot of people are getting filled with the Holy Spirit."

"Well, that's awesome."

So, when several days later Michael said he was going to meet with Pastor Kerry, I knew God had worked all these circumstances together. And as he drove home from their time together, he called me and told me how Pastor Kerry had prayed for him and that he started speaking in tongues.

"Can you believe that? Me? Speaking in tongues! Pastor also told me to get ready; God is about to bless the ministry He's given us in a major way."

So, when we spoke that next weekend, I decided to do as their pastor asked. I didn't talk about the dreams and visions that the Lord had given, not only to me, but to many others. I felt stifled and didn't like feeling that way. Later on that week when I ran into a few friends who knew the more intimate parts of my story, I was almost embarrassed by it—like it was weird or nonsensical.

Then, plainly I heard,

"Do not apologize for the way I operate."

In that moment, I decided I would not stifle the Spirit or His work. I would proclaim it boldly. After all, it wasn't me who had done these things. It was Him. And it was a good thing, because we soon received another call to share our story at a church.

CHAPTER 34

In the following months, God provided opportunities for Michael and me to speak in schools and churches. We even had the opportunity to share our story on several radio stations.

One afternoon, Michael went to Jonesboro trying to sell my children's products and trying to book more shows at churches. Later that day he came into the house and said, "I have a prophetic word for you. Come out here, so I can tell you." I went outside to the porch.

"What's up?"

"Okay, yesterday as I was driving around Jonesboro, I saw a banner that had Earl Bell on it." I didn't have a clue who that was, so Michael proceeded to tell me he was an Olympic athlete—a pole vaulter. Michael was also a pole vaulter in Memphis, where he was raised. And a state champion at that! "Okay, here is what you need to know about pole vaulting. Once you place your pole in the pit, you are committed to going over. I believe you did that when you went public with your story at Bott Radio in Memphis. The pole will start to bend, and as you start getting closer to going over the bar, you'll gain momentum."

I had shared my story on the radio network the previous week, so the word resonated with me. "Okay."

Then he added something that really caught my attention, "But if you go backwards, you're going to get hurt."

I sat there and let it sink in. "So, there's no turning back now," I thought as I gazed at the sun rising over the mountains.

I decided to start releasing excerpts from my book onto my blog. I started taking out Facebook ads and trying to get myself over the bar but knew there was no way it was going to happen without the power of the Holy Spirit. But, I also knew there was no turning back.

I believed my next step was to start telling people that John Grisham was the next to read my book and to ask them to help me get over the wall that had been placed before me.

"You know, I think I'm going to get friends of mine who have the faith and who know the story to help me get this message across," I said to Michael.

I thought social media was the way I should go, and I thought specifically of John Grisham's Facebook page. The next morning was Sunday. Again, Michael had been fasting, and he told me he had something for me.

"Last night I was up at 3:30 in the morning, and I couldn't sleep. So, I went outside and looked up a devotional on my phone. It was about Joshua at Jericho," he paused as he took out his phone to read it to me. After which, he said, "I agree with your idea about getting people to go with you to post your excerpts to John Grisham's Facebook page. I think that idea is from the Lord."

We talked about how Joshua and his army marched around the wall for six days, once a day, then on the seventh day, they marched seven times, blew the trumpet and God brought down the wall (Joshua 6). "You've been given a wall, but the Lord is about to take it down for you."

I prayerfully considered which people could help me with this special task and came up with several names. And when I thought about Joshua having an army of 40,000 (Joshua 4:13), the Lord spoke to my spirit,

"It's not the size of the army; it's the faith of the army."

I scrolled through my friends and wrote down names as they'd "pop" off the page to me. I started with about 50 names and sent each one a personal message about helping me write posts to John Grisham's Facebook wall. Some replied immediately with a "yes," and one replied with a "do you think that sounds like a good idea?" Some did not reply at all. In the end, I had about 25 people commit to helping me for seven days.

The plan was intact, the army was gathering, and the prayers were going forth. When I sent out the first message to the "army," and as I typed out the words, "John Grisham's Facebook wall," I thought the similarity between Joshua's wall and this wall was interesting.

A few nights later, I was walking around the courthouse square. I stopped to talk to a local pastor's wife, and she asked about my book. I told her I still believed it was for John Grisham (like I had told her a year prior), and then I told her about my plan to share a blog post about a miracle to his wall every day for six days. I trusted the Lord would show us what to do on the seventh day. While we were talking about Joshua at Jericho, another woman walked up and told me she had studied that story this past week. I didn't give her any details but listened to what she was saying. Before she walked off, she turned around, looked me in the eye, and said, "And may the wall fall for you."

Mr. Grisham,
Your greatest story is still to come. The Lord is drawing you to Himself.

Miracle #1 Caroline's First Vision

This was actually Caroline's first vision. After she had her second vision, a few months later, I decided to...

www.rachelsraft.com

One post from an "army" member

The first day of the "march," I opened my Facebook messages and was surprised to see two messages from friends saying they were ready to march. I'd posted the first post on my blog then copied it to each member. I asked them to share a few personal words, if possible, to make it more real to him. I wanted him to read them and see that there were people besides myself who believed in the book. The army surprised me. They went way beyond what I was expecting. So, we posted every day for six days. Then on the seventh day, we each shared seven posts about miracles from my blog. When the seventh day passed, I was relieved that the task was complete, but I did not see the wall "fall," so I did not know what to do.

I decided to pray and fast for three days.

CHAPTER 35

"Lord, please take a step towards me, please! A step! Anything," I cried out to Him. It had been ten days since I had released several posts and had asked an "army" to help me march the message forward.

Michael and I started a fast, and on the third day of the fast, I received a phone call from an old family friend. She was a retired schoolteacher in Texas and was aware of my story as she'd seen a few of my posts on Facebook.

"I have a story I want to share with you," she said as I took the call and walked out onto our porch. "I used to proofread and edit manuscripts on the side. But, you know, now that I am retired, I have not done that in years."

"Uh-huh," I said as I sat down on the rocking chair.

She continued, "So, last week I got a call out of the blue. It was a lady who was calling to ask if I would read and edit her manuscript. I told her I no longer edit manuscripts but thanked her for thinking of me. She continued on and said she really wanted me to edit and proof her manuscript. I told her I was retired and that I didn't do that anymore. But she was very persistent. She even went so far as to say she had asked her pastor for a recommendation, and he said to call me. I literally gave her a hundred reasons as to why I could not edit her manuscript, but she persisted. Finally, I relented and said, 'Okay,

211

I will read your manuscript. Read it. That is all, but I cannot proof it.'" She was pleased with that answer, so she said she would bring it to me."

She paused then continued, "She brought it to my house, and a few days later I sat down to read it. You know, I was sitting there in a chair in my living room—looking at the manuscript—noticing the title, feeling the thickness of it in my hands. Then all of a sudden, I had a vision."

"Yes, Lord," I thought, "You are taking a step towards me."

"As I was looking at the manuscript, the Lord gave me a vision of John Grisham. He was sitting on a chair holding your manuscript in his hands and reading it, just as I sat holding this woman's. Then I knew why all of this had come about. It was so the Lord could give me a vision for you. I thought of how I'd gotten the phone call out of the blue and why her pastor had told her to call me. It was for you. For you to know that he will read it, and for you to continue moving forward."

What could I say? It was so personal, so miraculous.

"Thank you, God. And thank you, Glenda. I have been praying and fasting for three days. This is the third day, and I was asking God to take a step towards me. He's done it."

"Rachel, I began to pray for you after the vision, and the Lord gave me the word 'persistent.' You need to continue to be persistent. Not only in your actions but in your spirit and in your prayers. Persistent."

I thanked her for her phone call and assured her it was an answer to prayer and fasting. And with her word and vision for me, I decided to continue to push forward until God delivered on His promises.

We started posting again, but by the sixteenth day, I was wondering if we were doing the right thing. Each morning I had prayed, "God, show me we are at the right place." I wondered if anyone was seeing them and if anyone was reading them. I wondered if they were reaching beyond the computer screen. I asked God to bless all my friends who were helping me and to show us we were doing what He wanted.

"Are we at the right place?

It was October 18th. I started reading Proverbs 18. I asked Him again, "Show me we are at the right place."

I looked down again at Proverbs 18 and found the very next verse, verse 11, which read:

"A rich man's wealth is his strong city, And like a high *wall* in his own imagination…" (NASB, emphasis mine).

I lifted my head up. "Yes, we are at the right place."

A few hours later, I went on Facebook to see how the posts were coming along, but I couldn't seem to make any of them come up on my phone. I walked into the bedroom and pulled it up on the computer. When I clicked on John Grisham's page, it said, "There are no posts to show." I called Michelle to see if it was just me or if the same happened to her.

"Let me pull it up…hmmm, mine says the same thing, 'There are no posts to show.'"

After almost two weeks of posts, I counted about 350 messages to John Grisham.

"Surely someone would notice that," I felt overwhelmed by the immensity of it all.

And now, I guess they had.

I started getting texts from the "army" about how they could no longer post, and before long, we discovered it was not that we had been blocked—all the posts from the last several years were down, and there was no way to write more.

My heart was not to embarrass John Grisham. My heart was to do what God had called me to do. And I had said over and over again how difficult it was. How stupid I must have looked. But, when the Holy Spirit moved, I either got in the direction He was going and went with Him or get out of the way. I decided to go with Him.

But still, I didn't hear anything.

Once again, days turned into weeks and weeks into months. Fall arrived, and Michael was working on a cruise ship while I was at home. One evening, Micah was scared so I took my pillow and went upstairs to the other twin bed in his room.

"Alright, buddy, I'm going to stay in here with you." We dozed off to sleep when suddenly I woke up drenched in sweat.

"Oh! What was that?"

I'd woken from a vivid dream. I sat up in bed and wiped the dampness from my neck and forehead. It was the first dream I'd had involving John Grisham.

In my dream, I was driving in a town, not Mountain View, but somewhere with rolling green hills. I'd heard he was doing a book signing at a store, and I was frantically trying to make my way to the signing before it was over. I didn't own any of his books, but I did have a Mountain View phone book in my car, so I pulled into the parking lot where he was, grabbed the phone book from behind the seat, and went in. There were a few people already in line ahead of me, and when I got to the front, I set the phone book in front of him. He said, "You're from Mountain View?"

"Yes," I replied.

Then I said three specific things to him: "Mr. Grisham, the Lord led me to your doorstep, literally to your family's dining table at church. I have a manuscript I've been trying to get into your hands for two years. It's the Lord's doing, and it's marvelous in our eyes" (Psalm 118:23).

"I'd like to read it," he said.

That's when I woke up.

Taking a deep breath, I grasped my hand as if the phone book were really there. I dabbed the sweat from my face and fanned myself with my hands.

"Good grief, it must be burning up in here."

Everyone was asleep, so I crept out of bed and quietly walked downstairs to where my phone was plugged in. I googled "book signings" and his name but read he hadn't done any in over twenty years, so I brushed it off as one more encounter outside of my reach.

Three months passed, and there was no word from John Grisham, his agent, or his family. Again, I questioned God. I started to doubt. I doubted so much that I woke up at night wondering what God was going to do.

The cruises ended for Michael, the holidays passed with much financial stress, and I wanted an answer. I was pregnant with our sixth child, and we were depending on God, once again and as always, for provision and for defense. Surrendering all these areas of my life was, for me, the ultimate step of faith.

One day I was waiting for Caroline during her dance practice, and I asked God for a verse. I opened to Isaiah: 63:12-13 and read, "…Who divided the waters before them to make for Himself an everlasting name, Who led them through the depths?" (NASB).

That is what I knew of God, but now I wanted to see the waters part. I wanted Him to part the sea and let me walk through. I wanted Him to do what was impossible for me but possible for Him.

At that time, persisting in prayer was one of the hardest things I had ever done. God had given specific instructions. We had followed them, and He shut up the heavens. He was silent. I trudged through, continuing with the hope to see Him move. Or move on with my life. But He didn't seem to let me do that. I was in a holding pattern. I often told friends that I wanted to press an "I don't care" button and move on, but God would not allow it. One friend suggested it was the Holy Spirit's way of helping me push through. For two years I'd been trying to give a book that I believed was a message from the Lord to John Grisham. No one could've ever convinced me my assignment would be so difficult.

To add to that, the theater's contract for Michael had him performing one day a week instead of two for just seven months out of the year. There was no way we could survive on half of what we'd been making. The cruise shows ended, too, and we started feeling it might be time to leave Mountain View. I couldn't imagine leaving in the condition we were in. We had nowhere to go, no jobs, and a baby arriving in June. But everything we read in the Bible and everything we sensed the Holy Spirit saying seemed to point that direction. It was late January, and I was reading about the parting of the Red Sea in Exodus 14:15-16.

"Then the Lord said to Moses, 'Why are you crying out to Me? Tell the sons of Israel to go forward. As for you, lift up your staff and stretch out your hand over the sea and divide it, and the sons of Israel shall go through in the midst of the sea on dry land'" (NASB).

"Go forward?" I laughed. I could imagine hundreds of thousands of Israelites standing on the verge of the Red Sea, toes in the water, inching in, deeper and deeper. And what did God say? To go forward. "How funny. Uh Lord, we are standing with our feet in the water and you want us to move forward?" It seemed ridiculous. Not unlike some of the things God had told me to do.

Wrestling with God one morning, I sat there wanting to hear from Him—the turmoil raging in my spirit over if He was going to bring about the delivery or not. I was listening to a sermon on my phone, and the preacher said sometimes people go several weeks without praying. I couldn't imagine. Not after where I'd been in my life. Wanting so badly to release this work from my hands, I was truly in distress.

Almost as if I could see the words being typed out on a typewriter, I saw in my mind,

"Unbelief is hindering your miracle."

If shackles could've fallen and chains could've broken, they would've. Perhaps they did. I picked up my journal, wrote it down, got on my face, and asked for forgiveness. I thought back to when Caroline had her vision of me standing at a book fair with my published book. She told me God didn't want me to believe because she believed, He wanted me to believe because I believed. And after all He had done, I still wrestled with doubt and wanted to be free from this calling on my life. The words sank down like morsels to the depth of my soul. I would have to change my pattern of thinking and trust God was going to do what He had said, whether I could see what He was doing or not. Sometimes faith is like that: not seeing past the end of my nose but pressing forward, one foot in front of the other, even in total darkness.

After homeschooling group that afternoon, Kiley, one of the kids' friends, came over to play. I'd made hot chocolate, and we were sitting at the dining room table stirring the marshmallows with our spoons.

She picked up a piece of paper. "Do you believe I can cut a hole big enough for you to walk through?"

"No." Micah and I said as we looked at each other.

She started to cut the paper. Back and forth she went, cutting for several minutes. She held it back up. "Now, do you believe you can walk through this?"

Our answer remained the same as she continued to cut.

After several more minutes, she held out a large, zig-zag shaped circle from the single piece of paper—large enough to walk through.

"Now do you believe I can?"

Micah stood up from the table and walked through the life-size circle cut-out.

Her red curls bobbed around her shoulders as she held it out with pride. "The last time I did this, I gave it to my grandad because he believed I could do it."

I turned around as I had already started clearing the table. "Wait, say that again."

"The last time I cut one of these out, I gave it to my grandad because he did not doubt I could do it."

I felt pressed to ask her, "So, what was significant about him not doubting you?"

She pushed her glasses closer toward her face. "Well, he's seen all the neat things I've done before, and he knew I could do it."

With those words on my mind, I thought of how I'd always believed God would take us back to Tennessee—that He would do miraculous things for us in Mountain View for a season then take us back home. And the more things continued to dry up, the stronger the conviction became. We were studying Jonah in Bible study, and I thought about how God had given Jonah instructions to go to another town. He didn't want to go, disobeyed, ran from God, got swallowed up by a fish, and was vomited onto dry land. Through it all, God's instructions remained the same: go to Nineveh.

Michael felt the same way: it was time to leave. But with so many questions, it was hard to take the step of faith. So, we continued to wait. I'd learned in Bible study that sometimes God didn't give steps two, three, or four if we hadn't obeyed at step one. That was how I felt. God had told us to leave, but we wanted to know the next steps first.

The kids went to stay with Michael's parents in Tennessee one weekend, and we were going to meet them halfway in Memphis for pickup. Christopher was with us, but I knew the drive would be easier if I could get a friend to keep him for the day. I texted one who replied she was sick, so I asked another friend. It was time to go, and I still had not gotten a message back. So, I strapped Christopher into the car seat and headed to get gas before getting on the highway. I checked my phone one more time, and sure enough, my friend had texted me thirty minutes prior.

"I'd love to keep him! Bring him over!"

I placed my phone back in my purse and the Holy Spirit whispered, *"I provided for you as you went."*

CHAPTER 36

A few nights later, I was reading in our bedroom when I heard, "BOOM!"

I heard it again.

Then I knew what it was. I raced to the living room window to see one last white, brilliant firework cascading across the sky.

"Oh, Jesus, you are with me."

I needed milk for the morning, so I asked Michael if I could go to the store.

"Yes, but we only have four dollars in the account, so that is all you can get."

By the time I was in the parking lot, I was crying. I was so tired of being in our situation. I called Michelle.

"It's okay. You can do this. You've done this before. Just go in there and get what you need. Let me pray for you."

When she was done, I wiped my cheeks, dried my eyes, and went in. I saw one person I knew—a pastor's wife—the same pastor who had been hired at the church in place of Michael.

"How are you?" I asked her as I forced a smile across my glistening face. They were expecting their third child and had decided to move to a different house. "What are you going to do with your boxes once you are finished with them?"

"Nothing," she replied. "Do you want them? You are more than welcome to have them."

"Yes, I'd love to have them. I'll text you."

Slowly, we started packing up our house. People started asking us where we were going, and we told them Tennessee, probably the Memphis area. We were in agreement it was time, and although we didn't know the specifics, we trusted God would show us. I wrote down every single promise God had given me and lined our doorframe with them.

"It's all I have," I said to Michael. "There's nothing else…only God's promises. That is all we are standing on." The night before we left, anxiety gripped my heart as I looked at the night sky through the bedroom window. What on earth were we thinking? Leaving with nowhere to

The doorframe and window lined with God's promises to me

go? No job? A baby on the way? Trying to rest, thinking through the pieces of paper that were lining our front door, I barely got any sleep that night.

We rented a U-Haul, loaded it, said our good-byes to our friends in Mountain View, and headed to Memphis. Once we arrived, we put all our things in storage and continued on to

Michael's parent's house in Nashville. That's when it hit me that this might be one of the stupidest things we'd ever done. Every night I woke up in a panic.

"We have no jobs, no place to live, and a baby coming in three months. How dumb."

Immediately I wished we hadn't done it. It was the biggest step of faith we had ever taken, and suddenly it felt like a mistake.

One morning after my shower, I locked the door, sat down on the floor, and cried until I couldn't cry one more tear.

"God, what have we done? Where are you? This is so stupid. I believe You told me You would provide as we went, but here we are—no job, no home of our own, and a newborn coming. This is a nightmare."

I cried so much and was in there for such a long time that my kids thought I had left.

"Mom, have you been at the grocery store?" Micah asked as I walked into the kitchen.

"Nope! I was just getting dressed."

Slowly, everyone started to look up at me from the breakfast table.

"I thought you went to the store or something. It seems liked you've been gone forever," he said again, pushing the subject.

"No. I've been here. Sometimes it takes girls a long time to get dressed," I said bluntly, hoping he would drop it. My heart was still raw with pain, and it was so hard to act like I was okay.

We started looking for rental homes, and Michael started looking for employment in Memphis. Two days before we were going to leave to look at houses, Michael received a call about a job he'd applied for before we left. He was being considered for a position in Mountain View, and the employer wanted to interview him. Our plans for looking for a place to live were suddenly placed on hold.

The sun was setting, dinner was over, the kids were playing, and Michael and I were sitting in his parents' living room. He was scrolling through the news on his phone when suddenly he stood up, "Oh my gosh, you're not going to believe this."

"What?"

"Guess who is doing a book tour after twenty five years of not doing them?"

I repositioned myself on the couch to look at him, "John Grisham?"

"Yep."

He started reading the article and rattling off the twelve cities John Grisham would be visiting—mostly northeastern, when he came to Nashville.[12]

"No way," I felt the sting of a tear in my eye. "No freakin' way...you've got to be kidding me."

---

[12] "John Grisham Returns to the Road for His First Tour in 25 Years!" *JGrisham*. Penguin-Random House. www.JGrisham.com.

"I'm not."

"When is it?"

"June 22nd."

"Two days after my due date." I picked my phone up off the table, "Do you think I should try to go?"

"Absolutely."

I thought back to when God had told me to *"Expect the delivery"* and had seen two deliveries taking place simultaneously. I googled the news article then decided to make the purchase for the book signing.

"Remember the dream I had about a book signing? But I knew John Grisham didn't do them anymore. Well, lookie lookie what God has done for me."

After a month of being at my in-laws, we were ready for a break. Michael called a pastor friend of his who had offered his retreat if we ever needed a place to stay. He told us to come for a week, so we loaded up the kids and went to Knoxville. I was still losing sleep over the fact that there were nine, soon to be ten, of us living under the same roof at my in-laws'. Michael was still unemployed. We'd sent out resumes and hadn't heard anything, and he still had not heard back about the job in Mountain View.

When we were ten miles from the pastors' retreat, our car started shaking. We drove the last ten miles at a snail's pace then coasted in to the retreat. It was a beautiful, 5,000 square foot house on fourteen acres. We had plenty of room to spread out, and the kids had space to run and play. The night we arrived, we asked Pastor Ray about a good mechanic in town, and he told us he'd call someone he knew in the morning.

"The Lord told me to give you $200 for groceries this week," he said as he pulled out his wallet. "I recently got a rebate on my car, so this isn't coming out of any particular account. And I'm going to pay for whatever you need fixed on your car. God gave me this money, and so I'm excited to help you guys out."

"Excited." I laughed to myself at his enthusiasm. "How precious."

The day we were supposed to leave, the starter in our car went out, as well. It kept us from going home, and on the morning we'd planned to leave, Michael walked into the bedroom and said, "I'm thinking about asking Pastor Ray if we can rent this house from him for a while. What do you think?"

"I would LOVE that…"

Later that night, I was putting Christopher to bed while Michael and the kids were taking a gift over to Pastor Ray and his wife. Michael prayed over asking Pastor Ray about renting the house, and we were all in agreement he should. I was praying and singing praise songs while he was gone, and when they returned, Michael told me that Pastor Ray agreed to rent the house for a small amount until the baby arrived. However, at some point we would have to decide where we'd go at the end of our stay.

I was overcome with joy.

"Provide as you go…"

I started calling doctors in the Knoxville area but could not find one that would take me at such a late state of pregnancy. So, I called a former doctor of mine just south of Nashville. At the end of May, we moved to Knoxville, and I commuted back

226

and forth for my appointments, a two hour drive. It made me quite nervous. Two weeks before my due date, I started having contractions, so I drove to Nashville to be seen and decided to stay until the birth of Kathleen.

I didn't know which would come first—the delivery of our baby or the delivery of the book, but they seemed to be coinciding. My blood pressure was rising, and the doctor was concerned. All of this was coming down on me, and at one point, it seemed unbearable. I continued to pray what I prayed when pregnant with Christopher, "Lord, pull me into your plan." I texted friends and asked for prayer for both deliveries. To my hairdresser in Mountain View, I messaged the latest update and said, "I need your prayers," to which she replied, "Oh girl!!! Holy Ghost goosebumps right here!!! I heard the word delivery!!!" I messaged Dana and in one paragraph explained the situation concerning Kathleen and her delivery and in the next paragraph, the book delivery. She replied, "Seriously not trying to ignore the first part of that text but I heard trumpets blowing as I read the second part."

The Kelley Eight, Micah, Michael, and Mary Manor; Camille, me holding Kathleen, and Caroline holding Christopher, June 15, 2017

Exactly one week before the book signing, Thursday, June 15th, my doctor decided to induce me. It was the shortest labor I'd ever had, and we welcomed precious Kathleen Rachel into the world. I decided by the time I gave birth for the sixth time, I could name her after myself!

We stayed three nights at the hospital then drove to our rental in Knoxville where I continued to add a few more pages to my manuscript. With my sixth child safely delivered, I anticipated the second part of my delivery—the delivery of a timely word to an earthly king.

The original manuscripts (there were two) printed and ready to be wrapped and delivered

And it happened just like God had said two years prior—I delivered our child and the manuscript in the same week. Exactly one week after I gave birth to Kathleen, I stood in line at Parnassus Book Store in Nashville to place my book in John Grisham's hands. I was not nervous, I was confident...and boy was I determined to leave the bookstore without the manuscript. I didn't care what took place—I told myself there was no way I was walking out of the bookstore with it still in my hands. In my dream, I'd said three specific things to John Grisham, so I'd written them on a card and taped it to the front of the gift.

When I got to the front of the line, we shook hands, introduced ourselves, and then I said, "Mr. Grisham, I met you a couple of years ago while living in Mountain View. I went to church with your parents, and they were always so nice to us and to our kids…"

"Oh, okay! What a small world. Mountain View is a pretty place, but you have to tell me…what on earth were you doing in Mountain View?"

I took a deep breath as I felt for the box inside my purse.

"Oh, you know, hanging out, raising a bunch of kids…"

Delivery Day at last! You can see the wrapped manuscript on the wooden bench behind us, June 22, 2017

He was very nice and personable as we talked about the small town, his family, and the theater where Michael entertained. I pulled the wrapped package out of my purse and said, "I have a gift for you, and I'll just set it right here," as I laid it on a chair behind him.

He signed my copy of *Camino Island*. Then before I walked off, he asked, "So, this is for me?" as he pointed at the gift.

"Yes," I replied, "that is for you." As I flipped through the pages of his book, I noticed the title of his final chapter was the same as mine: "The Delivery."

CHAPTER 37

The glass door closed behind me as the wind hit my face. Exhaustion seemed to finally take over every inch of my body. I walked toward our van as my shoes hit against the hot summer pavement.

Truthfully, I felt like crawling.

I felt like crawling and then perhaps falling on my face—maybe in gratefulness to the Lord or maybe to sob so hard I'd soak my navy blue dress.

It was finished.

But, I should have known.

I should have known when at my darkest and absolute lowest, God would perform miracles like a fireworks show and place a myriad of divine appointments, too numerous to count, in order to accomplish the seemingly impossible task.

I should have known when He told me to place a divine message in the hands of one of the greatest authors of our time, He would part the Red Sea (or at least, in my case, the Mississippi River) to set the final work into motion.

When He said, "John Grisham is the next one to read your book," He would be faithful to His word. When I thought it would never happen—God overcame.

I opened the door and fell into the passenger seat. My husband was holding our newborn, and the other five kids were talking over one another. "How'd it go, Mom? Did you do it? Did you deliver it to him?"

At that moment, joy overwhelmed me. Relief and exuberance broke through the weariness as the word "jubilee" came into my heart.

"Yes!" I exclaimed. "It's done!"

We stayed six more weeks in Knoxville at the pastor's retreat, and then we moved back to Arkansas where Michael was offered a position at a college. It was a good-paying job with benefits, and we were grateful for the financial blessing and stability that came with his employment. As far as myself, I felt certain the Lord wanted me to rest, so I enrolled the kids in school and stayed at home with the two little ones. And after two years of resting and waiting, I believed God wanted me to move forward with the publication of this book. I haven't heard from John Grisham. Yet. I still believe the Lord has a mighty plan to use John Grisham to bring many people to Himself. So, I will continue to pray and believe for God to bring that to pass. And perhaps this book will be a tool to do just that.

But even with that belief, I know that this path the Holy Spirit led me down was about many things. The Holy Spirit led me on a journey about obedience at any cost and about my God who calls me to follow Him wherever He may lead. My God, who is real and personal, is the God who works and speaks to His people, even today.

When I think back to the day I sat at that hosts' barstool, praying and envisioning a raft for Michael, I think about who I was at the time and what I would say to that girl, if I could.

I would tell her...

I would tell her about the unbelievable event God is going to do in her life. Tell her no matter how hard the storm beats against her or how low she has to fall before He pulls her out, she will be rescued. A mighty rescue. A rescue only God could give.

And when He does it, and He will, He will confirm everything He has ever told her.

Yes, that is what I would do...

I would tell her.

And perhaps in her years of praying for and expecting a raft for her husband, she would realize how God had sent one for her. Her very own raft:

Rachel's Raft.

Afterword

When this book was almost complete, the Lord put it on my heart to add this one, last part—the most important part in the manuscript. There is a Savior who is in love with you (John 3:16). If you want to follow Him today, you can. His name is Jesus.

The Bible says that "all have sinned and fall short of the glory of God" (Romans 3:23, NIV). Sin separates us from God, and Jesus came and died on a cross to pay for my sins and yours. There is only one way to God the Father, and that is through His son, Jesus (John 14:6). God has provided the way, but it is up to each of us to accept that gift. Salvation is a gift that He freely gives (Romans 6:23).

Here is how you can receive Christ:

1. Admit that you are a sinner (Romans 3:23).
2. Be willing to turn from your sins (Acts 3:19).
3. Believe that Jesus died on the cross and rose from the grave (Romans 10:9-10).
4. Through prayer, invite Jesus to come into your life and to fill you with the Holy Spirit (Romans 10:13).

You can pray this prayer:

Dear Lord Jesus, I know I am a sinner, and I ask for Your forgiveness. I believe You died for my sins and rose from the dead. I turn from my sins and invite You to come into my heart and my life. I want to trust and follow You as my Lord and Savior. Fill me with Your Holy Spirit. In Jesus' name, Amen.

To get to know Him better:

1. Get a Bible and read it every day—it is God's Holy Word and He will speak to you through it (2 Timothy 3:16).
2. Talk to God in prayer every day—it will transform your life!
3. Tell others about Christ—tell them what He has done for you.
4. Get into a church where the Bible is preached and the Holy Spirit moves!

Made in the USA
Columbia, SC
26 September 2019